I0458989

NEXT LEVEL
Woman

NEXT LEVEL
Woman

**Burn the Rulebook,
Build Your Empire**

Nevşah

NEXT LEVEL WOMAN
by Nevsah

First Edition
Copyright © 2025

Nevsah Institute

All rights reserved. No part of this publication
may be reproduced, distributed, or transmitted in
any form or by any means, including photocopying,
recording, or other electronic or mechanical
methods, without the prior written permission
of the publisher, except as permitted by U.S.
copyright law.

Paperback ISBN: 978-1-969679-11-7
Hardcover ISBN: 978-1-969679-12-4

For all the men I loved,
and for everyone who challenged me,
shut doors in my face, turned me down,
or tried to dim my fire. Thank you for
unknowingly sculpting the woman who
shines brighter than ever.

Contents

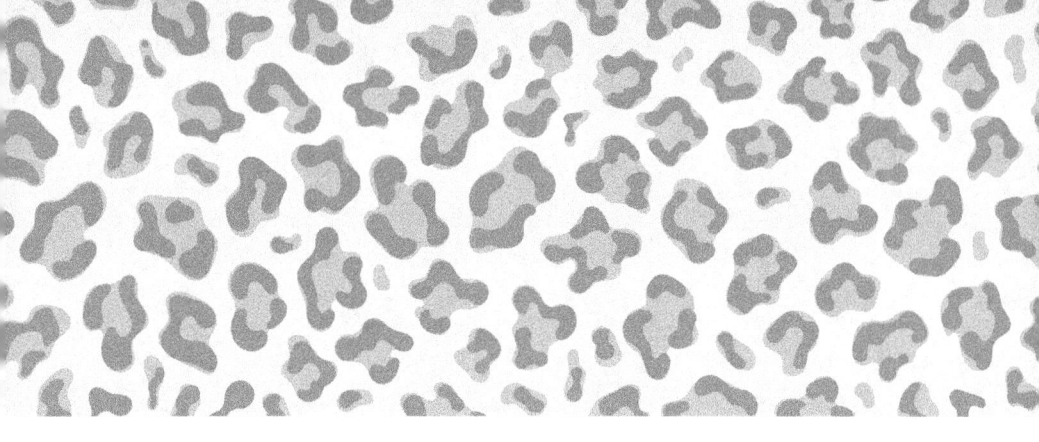

PART 1:

Women Are Different

Introduction

June 26, 1992. I am jolted awake on the cold, hard street; my body battered and broken. Through the haze of pain, a startling clarity hits me: "OK, I think I get the message now."

For months, the universe had been signaling me to slow down in every aspect of my life. But I'd been too caught up in my whirlwind of ambition to listen. Now, fate had forced me to a grinding halt. This moment marked a seismic shift in my life's trajectory. But to understand its true significance, let's rewind the clock.

I am a young girl growing up on the Turkish coast, opposite the Greek islands. My world is a vibrant tapestry of cultures—friends from France, Italy, and England, a family with Greek roots, and the privilege of an American college education in Izmir.

From day one, I am programmed for high performance. In my family, there is no such thing as can't or shouldn't. Every challenge is an opportunity, and I attack life at 300 percent. At four and a half, I dive into ballet, pushing through pain to perfect my craft. I am not just a dancer—I am a professional swimmer, a volleyball star, and a born leader in every arena. Success isn't just a goal; it is my oxygen. I don't know how to exist any other way. But here's the thing about living life in the fast lane—sooner or later, you're bound to crash. And crash I do, in spectacular fashion.

At seventeen, my relentless drive collides head-on with reality. In an instant, my world shattered. I find myself sprawled on the asphalt, my body a canvas of blood and broken glass. The pain is excruciating, but it pales in comparison to the shock of being forced to stop. What happened that day? What cosmic force finally made me slam on the brakes? The answer to that question would reshape my entire worldview. But first, I had to confront the hardest task of my life: learning to be still.

That summer, immobilized by injuries and bandages, I faced two months of enforced inactivity. For someone who had never known how to pause, it felt like an eternity. Yet in that stillness, I discover something profound: my relentless drive for performance has been a way of running from my true self.

Dear reader, how often do we push ourselves to the brink, filling every moment with activity, afraid to confront what lies beneath? It's time to ask ourselves: What are we really running from?

My journey of self-discovery led me down unexpected paths. I began exploring various spiritual traditions and philosophies, seeking answers to questions I'd never before dared to ask. Along the way, I uncovered truths about my conception, born into a family grappling with unimaginable trauma. These revelations became the foundation for a deeper understanding of my purpose in this world.

But let's pause here for a moment. I want you to reflect on your own life. Have you ever experienced a wake-up call? A moment that forced you to reassess everything you thought you knew about yourself? What messages might the universe be sending you that you're too busy to hear?

In the chapters that follow, we'll explore how to tune into these signals before life forces us to listen the hard way. We'll discover tools for self-mastery that allow us to live with purpose and intention, rather than being swept along by the current of our ambitions.

Are you ready to embark on this transformative journey, to peel back the layers of conditioning, and discover the radiant, powerful woman you were always meant to be? Then let's dive in. Your wake-up call awaits.

Spirit

In my early childhood, sometime between the ages of one and three, I remember waking up to see a tall, thin lady with curly hair in my room. I wasn't scared or threatened by not knowing who this person was. That's because I felt kindness and light coming from her. Whether she smiled at me or not, I'm not sure. Sometimes I would blink and she would be gone. But I saw her often. It's as if she was always there in some way, and I felt very connected to her. She was "My-lady-in-the-room." When I told my parents about this, naturally, they were worried. Looking back, I understand their fear-based conditioning, which unfortunately instilled fear in me too, despite having no reason to be afraid of this figure.

Shortly after, my parents decided I should take psychiatric medication even though I was just a toddler. Sadly, and perhaps unsurprisingly, I was on this medication for a couple of years, and I stopped seeing the lady.

Fast forward to 1992, when I was forced to stop and become more aware of myself, I began questioning my life's purpose and started practicing meditation and breathwork techniques. Through these practices, I began to reconnect with the woman from my childhood visions. In my meditations, the woman visited me and explained to me that because I was so young, I couldn't carry the inner wisdom I possessed on my own. She visited me over the years and I felt like she was a protective force in my life, almost like a guardian angel. But I was to discover eventually, she was not an angel. Nevertheless, I have felt her protective force my entire life.

Since then, I've become a Vedic meditation teacher and a globally recognized expert in breathing sciences and breathwork. I dedicate two to three hours daily to deep thinking, breathwork, and meditation, a practice I've maintained for about fifteen years. This consistent practice has led me to a state of consciousness where I'm not bound by time and space. I can connect with what Deepak Chopra calls the "timeless mind."

In this state of consciousness, which I believe many awakened beings and teachers connect with, and which is available to all of us as human beings, I can access any point in time and space. Using these breathing and meditative techniques, I've been able to connect with my baby self and other versions of myself throughout time. In return, this ability has helped me understand that my earlier life of constant performance and action was a way of disconnecting from my true self and capabilities.

As a woman, I've discovered that through meditation, breathwork, and what I refer to as the five principles of mastering the art of being a woman, one can transcend the limitations of the universe and connect with a timeless, universal reality. This reality is deeply connected to our divine nature and our connection with God. Just as our bodies can create life, we can directly connect with the creative force beyond the universe, space, and time.

However, my journey from being a constant performer to discovering this deeper truth wasn't easy. In my early twenties, I felt lost and purposeless. Unfortunately, one life-altering event wasn't enough for me to change my ways. Nevertheless, life kept sending me strong messages to stop and connect with my true self. I had multiple incidents—another car accident, this time, with my first husband, and a ceiling crashing on my head—all pushing me to stop and listen. I now understand that these intense experiences were directly related to the power and intensity of my life's mission—to help humanity connect with an unconditional mindset. But the more I refused to stop and connect with my true purpose, the more life threw these incidents at me, as if saying: "Just stop. Let go of this material world. Stop the acting, stop the performing."

It took me a couple of years, but I finally got the message. I began searching for methods to truly connect with myself and my purpose, leading me to where I am today.

Why is life like this? By the time of the last life-altering event, I experienced a profound inner awakening, but it was at odds with the external world I had created. I discovered there was a transformative energy within me, capable of impacting tens of thousands of people, which

I've harnessed over the past twenty years. However, I wasn't strong enough at the time to hold space for this energy, for who I truly was. In response, I built a huge wall around myself during the first twenty or so years of my life. This wall grew thicker and thicker with each performance and each achievement. The more I did, the more I was on the go, and the thicker this wall became. But all it did was hide my light and conceal the unconditional connection I had inside my being.

Growing up in the westernmost part of Turkey, I was raised in a bubble of Western ideals. Imagine this: 95 percent of the country is steeped in Eastern traditions, and I was a cultural anomaly. The pain of not belonging was a constant, silent companion. When I first ventured to Istanbul, that cosmopolitan melting pot, I felt the full weight of my otherness. As I met the eyes of my Eastern-minded compatriots, a crushing realization hit me: I don't belong here. This wasn't just culture shock; it was an identity crisis. There I was, a young woman in my early twenties, born into a Westernized bubble, suddenly confronted with a world that didn't match my upbringing. Where do I fit in? It was like growing up on a different planet and then being dropped into the "real" Turkey. This disconnect ran deep. My family's diverse heritage of Greek roots, Scandinavian blood, and Balkan influences set us apart in a predominantly Middle Eastern country. We weren't religious in a deeply spiritual land. I spoke the language, sure, but the mindset? It was foreign to me.

After the 1992 incident, when I started to slow down,

an awakening slowly began within me. But I didn't know how to break through that wall I'd built. In my early twenties, my inner experience was the complete opposite of my outer reality. Everything in my world—my marriage, friends, business—was misaligned with who I was becoming inside. This pain of not feeling like I belonged wasn't just a burden—it was a calling. I realized I was placed in this unique position for a reason: to be a bridge, a reformer, an agent of change. This is why I'm so passionate about empowering women, especially in the Middle East. It's why I lead projects helping women build businesses, find independence, and break free from limiting beliefs. My story, my pain, my mission—they're all interconnected. Dear reader, when you read the stories and ideas in this book, know that they come from a place of deep understanding. They're born from the struggle of straddling two worlds and finding purpose in that liminal space.

As my inner awakening accelerated and I gained clarity about myself and my purpose, I began practicing breathwork. This practice helped crack open the wall I had built. It was then that my journey as a teacher truly began. I had to learn to hold the light, to gain the strength to be the light, and to stay as the light. My path as a teacher started after I was able to break through that wall and allow my inner light to shine. It was a process of not only discovering my true self but also gathering the courage to embody and express it in the world. That's because I was deeply connected to the vision of the curly-haired woman I saw as a small child. That connection has always been there and remains strong today. She has provided me with an innate wisdom that has kept me calm and steady, no matter what happens in my life.

I have had several additional life-altering incidents over the years. One time, I found a gun pointed at my head. I don't remember panicking. This calmness, I believe, comes from my connection to a higher level of consciousness. It reflects the future me, but it's not just the future me—it's the true me. And this can be true for you, too. As you hold this book in your hands, seeking self-mastery, know that this wisdom and calm are within you, ready to guide you through any challenge.

From a young age, my world was steeped in mysticism. My grandmother, a devoted Sufi, planted the seeds of spiritual curiosity in my impressionable mind. Sufism, much like the Kabbalah, is the mystical heart of Islam, a path that transcends rigid religious structures to embrace a more liberated form of spirituality. This early exposure ignited a passion in me for understanding the human experience. By my early teens, I was devouring philosophical and spiritual texts with an insatiable hunger. At fourteen, you'd find me poring over Schopenhauer, wrestling with life's big questions. "Why is the world like this?" I'd ask, again and again, following each why to its logical conclusion. And you know what? This relentless questioning led me to a profound realization—the ultimate answer to all these whys was simply, because I am present. It's like peeling an onion, layer by layer until you reach the core of your own existence.

For over a decade and a half, I've embarked on a quest

to deepen this understanding. I've sought out wisdom from an eclectic mix of teachers across esoteric and mystic traditions—Sufis, shamans, Kabbalists, and more. Each encounter has added a new dimension to my spiritual toolkit.

✦

Until the twenty-first century, most of the awakened souls—those often called messiahs—have been men. But it's not because women aren't connected or capable. It's because we've been living in a man's world. This is a profound truth. Women are fundamentally different from men. We give birth; our bodies create life in a way men's bodies do not. Men operate with 70 percent male energy, which dominates our world. This energy makes their experience of the world highly physical. For example, when choosing a partner, men often prioritize physical attraction because their experience is rooted in the five senses.

Women, however, can connect with someone beyond physical appearance. We experience life with our eyes closed, so to speak, deeply attuned to the spiritual. Seventy percent of a woman's energy is spiritual, leading to a profound connection with the Divine, the Creator, and creation itself. This connection allows women to give birth, but it also means we don't engage with the material world in the same way men do. When I receive messages from the Divine, my connection is beyond physical reality, beyond the universe itself. It is a connection filled with immense wisdom, silence, light, and love that defies description.

Men's awakening processes are different. Even male meditation teachers, while achieving profound states, remain tied to the experience of the five senses, time, and space. Their connection with light and love is there but not as immersive as that of women. This difference is also reflected in sexual experiences. Men's orgasms are more physically connected, whereas women can transcend their physical bodies, experiencing something far deeper. This spiritual strength translates to physical resilience.

I have two daughters, both born naturally. My second birth was especially rapid, happening in just twenty-five minutes without an epidural. My body endured incredible pain, literally tearing apart in those minutes, yet I remained strong. I remember the intense pain and breathing throughout that day. No painkillers—nothing. In that moment, I told myself, "I'm immortal. I'm not just a mortal being." Perhaps you think I was being grandiose, but I felt completely free from my body because if I had been even 1 percent connected to it, I might have succumbed to the pain. Again, this ability to endure pain comes from the fact that women are not as tied to the physical senses and material world as men are. This experience underscores the unique strength and connection women have with the Divine and the physical world.

Men experience the world through the five senses at about 70 percent, whereas women experience it at 30 percent. That's because women are 70 percent connected to the spiritual realm, which is filled with silence and love. When I meditate, all I feel is bliss—something that's hard to

put into words. Men, being more connected to the material world, can structure and articulate their experiences.
However, for a woman, expressing her light and love requires
being in her presence. Men can write books and materialize
their experiences, but women embody the womb energy
that transcends time and space (and write books too of
course!). This energy is deeply connected to the heart.

Historically, men have been prophets who bring wisdom and knowledge into structured forms, while women
have been healers and life-givers. We touch and heal, bring
forth life, and elevate the energies around us. The depth
of spirituality a woman on her journey can experience is
unparalleled. Any book written by a man on spirituality is
just a fraction of the truth—a mere 1 percent of the profound connection a woman can have with the Divine.

I smile at this realization. It's challenging for men to
accept because of their material power and evolved egos.
But as a woman connected with the Creator, I give life.
I've witnessed many miracles in my sessions with people.
Women who couldn't conceive became pregnant after a
twenty-minute breathing session. People with cancer have
experienced healing through touch. I'll discuss more of this
later in the book. Overall, this is the power of the feminine—bringing life, healing, and utilizing profound spiritual
connection.

Yet whatever insights men may bring through their
prophecies and experiences, they cannot fully relate to
a woman's experience. That's what I strive to convey to
women—you don't know the power you possess. Until you

stop and connect with that life energy, you won't realize your true potential. This is happening because it's a man's world, with structures and systems created by men. Women, being more adaptable, have had no choice but to fit into this framework. Over centuries, women have forgotten how to meditate, practice breathwork, and harness their spiritual power. We've spent more time in the material world, utilizing man-made systems, and in the process, we've forgotten our ability to give life, to heal, and to bring light and love. We've therefore become more like men, losing touch with our innate power.

Women on the journey of reclaiming their power must learn to use their male energy appropriately. Instead of using it to engage with the world like men, we need to use it to withdraw, to reconnect with ourselves and our spiritual strength. This is exactly what I teach. Women have lost their way by misusing their male energy to act like men—going out, achieving, and striving—rather than harnessing it to find their inner power. Don't get me wrong, there is nothing wrong with achieving and succeeding in the material world. I want you to do that. But I want you to first reconnect with your sacred female energy. Then your power will be tenfold and more than anything you could have previously imagined.

Many women around the world suffer because of this disconnect. In this book, you are going to discover your unique journey to realizing your full potential as both a woman and a human. That's because if I maintain my natural state as a woman, my body and psychology remain healthy. It's as if I have this incredible channel that lights up from within. When I stay connected to this power, this light, and this healing energy, it doesn't just affect me. It extends to everyone around me—my children, my husband, my colleagues. It's almost as if they can't get sick when I'm in this state. This is our natural balance as women. Likewise, the more I connect with my love and spirit, the more healing energy flows through me and into my surroundings—my family, my city, and even my country. It's a ripple effect of love and healing.

I believe that if every woman around the world could tap into this power and maintain this connection, we wouldn't see the level of war and chaos that exists in our world today. Our innate healing and nurturing energy could transform society on a global scale. This is the profound impact of a woman fully embracing her natural state and allowing her inner light to shine. It's not just about personal well-being, but about creating a harmonious and peaceful world for all.

The purpose of this book is to remind women that building structures and systems is primarily the domain of men. This is how they operate, function, and achieve results. Men are manifestors. They build, plan, and take action in our system. This is how they go to the moon, construct buildings, and create order. However, if we women solely operate in this manner, we risk losing our authentic system. As a woman, I don't function entirely in the material world. It's as if men, with their energy, have built the structures, for example, like the buildings in Manhattan. But women are like the wind flowing through these buildings. If I, as the wind, lose my ability to flow, bend, and bring life and air to these buildings, there would be no fresh air in Manhattan. There would just be buildings, and people would suffocate. The man-made structures are wonderful, but if I forget my role and think I should be building those buildings as well, trying to conform to that structure leads me to forget who I am.

We, as women, embody this creative power. We are the life-giving wind that breathes vitality into the world's rigid structures. Our role isn't to mimic male energy but to infuse it with movement, nurturing, and transformative force. This is our unique contribution, our authentic way of being. By embracing this truth, we not only maintain our essential nature but provide the balance our world so desperately craves. Our power lies in fully expressing our feminine essence, not in imitating masculine traits.

But here's the crucial part: this spirit, this energy, this essence, it doesn't exist in some abstract realm. It lives and breathes in our physical bodies. Our bodies are the vessels through which this feminine power flows and manifests in the world. Think about it. How often have you felt a gut instinct, a physical reaction to a situation before your mind could process it? That's your body speaking, channeling this innate wisdom.

As we transition to the next chapter, I want you to shift your awareness to your physical self. Feel the power coursing through your veins, the strength in your muscles, the wisdom in your cells. Your body is not just a shell. It's an integral part of your feminine essence, a key to unlocking your full potential.

Sacred Reminders

✦ Your connection to the Divine and Creation is your birthright as a woman. You possess 70 percent spiritual energy that allows you to experience reality beyond the physical senses.

✦ Your inner wisdom and intuitive knowing are not your imagination—they are your direct line to truth. Trust what you feel and know from within.

✦ The power to heal, nurture, and transform exists naturally within you. When aligned with your feminine essence, this power flows first to heal yourself, then radiates outward to heal others.

✦ Your role is not to build rigid structures like men but to be like the wind—flowing, bending, bringing life and vitality to those structures. Don't lose your authentic nature trying to operate in masculine ways.

✦ Your body is not separate from your spirit. Rather, it is the sacred vessel through which your feminine power manifests in the world. Honor the wisdom that lives in your physical form.

Body

Everything in the universe is energy. Every single thing has its own electromagnetic field, and we daily experience these electromagnetic waves journeying throughout our bodies and through the world. Everything, including our bodies, is composed of this energy.

In reality, time and space are not absolute; they are perceptions of humankind. What truly exists is energy and light, which make up the electromagnetic fields that flow through us.

When we carry more judgments and distorted perceptions, we tend to live more deeply in the illusion or reality of time and space. We become trapped in a perceived reality, a physical reality. However, when we expand our consciousness and tap into light and love, which is an equilibrium level of the mind in our consciousness, we begin to transcend this illusion. In this expanded state, we tend to feel the physical body differently. We experience vibrations at a higher frequency, which can also be called gamma frequencies.

Gamma frequency is the highest level of frequency we can experience in the human body.

This shift in perception and vibration allows us to move beyond the limitations of our physical reality and connect with the deeper, more fundamental energy that underlies all existence. It's a way of experiencing the world that's more aligned with the true nature of the universe, beyond the constructs of time and space that our minds typically impose. By understanding and working with these energies, we can begin to transcend our everyday perceptions and tap into a more expansive, interconnected reality. This is the power of expanding our consciousness and aligning ourselves with the fundamental energies of the universe.

Let's explore the profound connection between our consciousness and our physical form. Our bodies are not mere vessels; they're intricate energy systems that respond to every nuance of our thoughts and emotions. The way we experience our physical reality is deeply intertwined with our level of awareness. Consider this: The more attuned you become to your body, the more your consciousness condenses into a tangible form. It's as if we're all part of a vast electromagnetic field, and our bodies are the points where this energy becomes most concentrated and real. This is the essence of practices like yoga and meditation. Far from being simple exercise routines, these are ancient technologies designed to align body and mind. They aim to achieve a perfect equilibrium, much like the ideal 7.4 pH balance in chemistry.

Have you ever wondered why balance poses in yoga can be so challenging? They're not just testing your physical strength; they're working with the subtle energy field that surrounds us. When you find stillness in these poses, you're not only stabilizing your body but also calming the turbulence in your mind. That's because there's a direct correlation between mental chaos and physical discomfort. It's no coincidence that the word disease breaks down to dis-ease. Every ailment in our bodies reflects an imbalance within our broader being.

But here's where it gets exciting: As you elevate your consciousness and move toward self-mastery, your relationship with your body naturally evolves. You begin to gravitate toward practices that nourish both body and soul—yoga, nutritious foods, and enlightening literature. It's not about forcing yourself into a health regimen. Rather, it's about aligning with habits that support your highest self.

I invite you to view your body through this new lens. It's not just a physical form; it's a finely tuned instrument capable of extraordinary feats. As we harmonize mind and body, we tap into the limitless energy field that surrounds us all. Are you ready to unlock this profound connection and discover the vitality and power that reside within you? Let's delve deeper into the wisdom of the body.

Letting Go

I often see an image while meditating: light shining outward, and as it does, my consciousness expands. This is what I associate with gamma frequency. In this state, there is no time, no space. We don't experience ourselves as confined to our physical bodies. Instead, we tend to connect with the eternal part of ourselves, tapping into a deeper meaning of life, our deeper mission, and our deeper purpose. In this expanded state, we transcend the limitations of our everyday perceptions. We touch something vast and timeless, something that goes beyond our individual selves and connects us to the greater whole of existence.

However, the more judgments and biases we hold, the more we become trapped in the episodic memories stored in our brains. These mental constructs pull us away from this expansive state. We start experiencing more of the illusions of time and space, becoming more entrenched in our limited, physical reality. It's as if our judgments and biases act like weights, tethering us to a more constrained way of experiencing the world. They keep us bound to our personal histories and individual perspectives, preventing us from accessing that higher state of consciousness where we can perceive the deeper truths of existence.

This contrast highlights the importance of releasing our judgments and biases, of quieting the constant chatter of our everyday minds. By doing so, we open ourselves to experiencing these higher frequencies, allowing us to touch that eternal part of ourselves and connect with our true purpose in life. That's because what we experience in the physical plane is directly tied to our level of consciousness. While everyone has a physical body, our experience of it varies greatly depending on our state of awareness. For example, someone with a lower level of consciousness tends to experience more weight, heaviness, and a stronger pull of gravity. It's as if their energy is more condensed, which in turn shrinks their consciousness. This creates a cycle—the more condensed the energy, the more the consciousness shrinks, and vice versa.

This condensing of energy and shrinking of conscious-ness is largely due to our preconditioned judgments. These judgments act like filters, coloring our perception of real-ity and limiting our ability to experience the world in its fullness. The more judgments we carry, the more our con-sciousness tends to contract. It's important to understand that this isn't just a mental phenomenon. It has real, physi-cal effects on how we experience our bodies and the world around us. Those with expanded consciousness often report feeling lighter, more connected, and less bound by physical limitations.

This perspective highlights the profound impact our inner state has on our outer experience. By working to release our judgments and expand our consciousness, we can literally change how we experience the physical world. It's a reminder of the power we have to shape our reality through our inner work and spiritual growth. That's because we possess an incredible power within our minds to either condense or expand energy. When we vibrate in judg-ments and remain fixated on the physical world, we tend to condense our energy. However, we also can expand that energy and transcend the limitations of the physical world we experience when our energy is condensed.

People who experience low frequency often feel a sense

of heaviness, as if they're carrying a great burden. This is why we hear expressions like "I have too much weight on my shoulders." It's not just a figure of speech—it's an accurate description of what's happening energetically. When someone experiences this kind of weight, it often indicates that they're holding onto too many judgments. These judgments act like anchors, pulling us down and making us feel heavy in both body and spirit. They keep us tethered to a denser, more limited experience of reality.

On the other hand, when we release these judgments and expand our consciousness, we often feel lighter and more free. We begin to vibrate at a higher frequency, which allows us to experience reality beyond the confines of the physical world. As such, this understanding gives us a powerful tool for transformation. By consciously working to release our judgments and expand our energy, we can change how we experience ourselves and the world around us. We can move from a state of heaviness and limitation to one of lightness and possibility.

It's a reminder that our inner state profoundly affects our outer experience. By cultivating awareness of our energy and consciously choosing to expand it, we can transform not just our perception, but our entire lived experience. That's power.

Our Bodies in Space and Time

How we experience our body and physical reality varies greatly depending on our level of consciousness. A wide swath of humanity all around the world experiences the world through a time and space illusion. This leads them to perceive time as distinctly divided into past, present, and future. But because they're so deeply embedded in their physical bodies and this linear perception of time, most people live their daily experiences without a broader vision or purposeful planning. They're caught up in what I might call "just living," which is just existing day to day without a deeper connection to their purpose or the greater flow of life. This mode of existence keeps us tethered to the physical plane, often preventing us from accessing higher states of consciousness or realizing our full potential. We're so focused on navigating the immediate demands of our perceived reality that we miss out on the expansive possibilities that come with a more awakened state.

It's like we're watching a movie of our life, scene by scene, without realizing we have the power to step back and see the entire story—or even to rewrite the script. We can be so caught up in the illusion of time and space that we don't realize there's a reality beyond these constructs. This perspective isn't meant to judge but to highlight the transformative potential that comes with expanding our consciousness. By recognizing the illusory nature of our everyday perceptions, we open ourselves to a more profound, more connected way of being in the world. We can move beyond just living to truly thriving by aligning ourselves with our deeper purpose and the greater flow of existence.

It's also important to recognize that the more condensed our consciousness becomes, the more fear we build up. This condensing leads to a lower frequency in both mind and body. When the mind and body are disconnected, the link between them weakens, which is intimately tied to fear—the fear of time, and the physical experience of life and death through our five senses.

Balancing

Various practices such as yoga and meditation aim to bring the body and mind into alignment. These practices recognize the fundamental connection between our mental and physical states and work to harmonize them. For example, when there's an imbalance, either a positive or negative charge in our electromagnetic fields, our energy becomes wobbly. This instability manifests in both our mental and physical states. It's like trying to maintain a balanced pose in yoga—the more scattered our thoughts, the harder it is to find physical equilibrium.

I've observed this firsthand as a yoga teacher. People who were more lost in their minds struggled to maintain balance in their physical bodies. The charges in the brain and distorted perceptions in the mind directly impact our physical state. If you have a chaotic mind, you'll likely have an unbalanced body. Once you lose balance in the mind, you lose it in the body as well. You may have encountered this wobbly energy in people you don't trust or feel uncomfortable around. The more distorted the mind becomes, the more unstable the body and the physical environment appear.

This interconnection between mind and body highlights

the importance of practices that promote balance and alignment. By working to calm our minds and align our thoughts, we can achieve greater stability and balance in our physical bodies. It's a reminder of the profound connection between our inner state and our outer experience, and the power we have to influence both through conscious practice and awareness.

Yoga is a wonderful practice to complement this journey of the mind. But do not worry if you do not live near a yoga studio or have money for classes. All you need is a mat (preferably) and there are many yoga classes you can do for free on YouTube as well as myriad apps that can lead you through a practice.

Many people believe that by practicing yoga or adopting these habits, they can achieve self-mastery. But in reality, it's the other way around. When you reach a state of self-mastery, you naturally gravitate toward these practices. It's your expanded consciousness that leads you to seek out yoga, not yoga that leads you to an expanded consciousness. When you attain self-mastery, you start doing yoga because you recognize its value for your body and mind. You begin eating healthier because you understand the importance of nourishing your body properly. You find yourself drawn to books that support your visions because your expanded awareness seeks further growth and alignment. These practices and habits are the outward manifestations of an objective mindset and a wise human being. They're not the path to wisdom, but rather the natural expressions of it. It's a subtle but crucial distinction.

This perspective shifts our focus from external actions to internal growth. Instead of trying to force ourselves into certain habits or practices, we can work on expanding our consciousness and developing self-mastery. As we do so, we'll find ourselves naturally drawn to activities and choices that support our higher state of being. Overall, it's a reminder that true transformation comes from within. By focusing on our inner growth and self-mastery, we naturally align ourselves with practices and habits that further support our evolution and well-being.

Sacred Reminders

✦ Your body is not just a physical form but an intricate energy system that responds to every thought and emotion. As you expand your consciousness, your experience of your body transforms.

✦ The more judgments you carry, the heavier your physical experience becomes. Release your judgments to experience more lightness and freedom in your body.

✦ Physical ailments often reflect inner turbulence. When you find peace within, your body naturally moves toward balance and healing.

✦ True transformation flows from the inside out. Rather than forcing external changes, focus on expanding your consciousness, and healthy habits and practices will naturally follow.

✦ Your body's wisdom runs deeper than the five senses. Learn to listen to this deeper knowing rather than being trapped in physical perceptions.

✦ Balance in the body mirrors balance in the mind. When you find stillness in thought, physical equilibrium becomes natural.

✦ Remember, you don't need elaborate practices or expensive programs to begin this work. Simple awareness and the willingness to turn inward are your most powerful tools for transformation.

Brain

As women, we often feel as if we are operating in a different realm than men. We have different instincts, intuitions, and urges and, at times, it can be frustrating trying to interpret and understand the actions of men. Of course, most of these differences can be chalked up to gendered societal expectations, but it's worth questioning whether there are more fundamental differences that influence our gendered experiences.

The question whether men's and women's brains are fundamentally different is a decades-long debate underscored by controversy and skepticism in the world of neuroscience. There is no such thing as the female brain or the male brain, but advances in brain imaging and artificial intelligence have provided evidence that male and female brains exhibit distinct patterns of organization and function and minor physical variations. Although these are subtle differences, they are significant enough to impact cognitive abilities, emotional processing, and vulnerability to neuropsychiatric disorders.

In *The Gendered Brain*, cognitive neuroscientist Gina Rippon argues that claims of significant brain differences between men and women, such as exaggerated differences in gray and white matter, are based on flawed research practices, including misinterpretation and publication biases and that they perpetuate misleading stereotypes about cognitive abilities.[1] While there are slight differences between male and female brains, these are primarily due to brain size rather than sex or gender. A comprehensive meta-synthesis of brain imaging studies found that size-related differences, such as women having smaller brains with a slightly higher ratio of gray matter, do not account for behavioral differences like empathy or spatial skills.[2] Rippon challenges the notion of a fundamentally different "female brain" and claims that behavioral and interest differences between genders are more influenced by cultural factors than by inherent biological differences.[3]

Findings suggest that behavioral sex differences are, to some extent, related to sex differences in brain structure but that this is mainly driven by differences in brain size, and causality should be interpreted cautiously.[4] However,

1 Eliot, L. (2019). Neurosexism: The myth that men and women have different brains. https://doi.org/10.1038/d41586-019-00677-x

2 Rosalind Franklin University of Medicine and Science. (2021, March 29). Massive study reveals few differences between men's and women's brains. *ScienceDaily*.

3 Eliot, L. (2019). Neurosexism: The myth that men and women have different brains. https://doi.org/10.1038/d41586-019-00677-x

4 van Eijk, L., Zhu, D., Couvy-Duchesne, B., Strike, L. T., Lee, A. J., Hansell, N. K., Thompson, P. M., de Zubicaray, G. I., McMahon, K. L., Wright, M. J., & Zietsch, B. P. (2021). Are Sex Differences in Human Brain Structure Associated With Sex Differences in Behavior?. *Psychological Science*, 32(8), 1183–1197.

structural differences between male and female brains do exist. In 1998, Stanford professor of psychiatry, behavioral sciences, and neurobiology, Nirao Shah, launched an investigation using advanced molecular techniques and uncovered real differences in brain structure demonstrating that, while these differences do not imply superiority or reinforce stereotypes, they are indeed present. For instance, women generally excel in verbal tasks and fine motor skills whereas men tend to perform better in visuospatial tasks. These cognitive differences are supported by anatomical findings from the University of California in Irvine professor of neurobiology and the Behavior School of Biological Sciences, Larry Cahill, who identified that women have a larger hippocampus, which impacts learning and memory, while men have a larger amygdala, which affects their emotional experiences. Additionally, brain-imaging studies reveal that women's brains show more coordinated activity between hemispheres, whereas men's brains exhibit more localized coordination, potentially influencing emotional memory and behavioral patterns.[5]

Further supporting these findings, research from a 2024 Stanford Medicine study utilized artificial intelligence to analyze brain activity in approximately 1,500 young adults and discovered that male and female brain activity patterns at rest were distinctly different, with no overlap. The study also found that brain connectivity patterns could

5 Goldman, B. (2022, September 21). *How men's and women's brains are different*. Stanford Medicine Magazine. https://stanmed.stanford.edu/how-mens-and-womens-brains-are-different/

predict cognitive functions like intelligence within each sex but not across sexes, suggesting fundamentally different determinants of cognitive functions between male and female brains.[6]

Overall, these studies underscore that sex plays a tangible role in brain structure and function. Still, it's important to keep in mind that sex differences in brain function are not absolute. These sex-related differences shouldn't be acknowledged to further enforce cultural stereotypes or expectations. Instead, this newfound understanding offers new insights into how biological factors interact with cultural influences to shape behavior.

But What Does it All Mean?

The intricate workings of our brains reveal fascinating distinctions between men and women. For men, discipline is key. It's no coincidence that many spiritual and religious practices were developed by men as these systems provide the structure and repetition that the male brain craves. This disciplined approach helps men stay focused, aligning their actions with their intentions and ultimately mastering their chosen paths.

Now, let's turn our attention to the female brain and its marvel of creativity and expansive energy. Imagine your mind as a universe unto itself, constantly expanding, generating new ideas, and exploring all directions of

---

6 Sax, L. (2024, May 24). *New research finds huge differences between male and female brains.* Psychology Today. https://www.psychologytoday.com/us/blog/sax-on-sex/202405/ai-finds-astonishing-malefemale-differences-in-human-brain

life simultaneously. This is the power of feminine energy—
ever-creating, ever-expanding. But with this incredibly
creative force comes a unique challenge. Our brains, much
like our energy, tend to scatter. We can become overwhelmed by the sheer volume of thoughts and ideas swirling
within us. It's as if our minds are reaching out to touch the
edges of the universe, constantly pushing boundaries.

A dear friend of mine recently immersed herself in an
important project for nearly two months. Her creative
energy was in overdrive, thoughts and ideas flowing non-
stop. The result? She experienced migraine attacks for the
first time in her life. This is a perfect example of what happens when we don't balance our expansive energy with
grounding practices.

You see, within us lies a powerful magnetic center—our
womb. This energy center has the potential to ground and
magnetize our creative forces. But when we neglect to
pause, to gather and ground this energy, we can experience physical symptoms like headaches or that feeling that
our brain might explode from overactivity. Sound familiar?
Understanding this dynamic is crucial for harnessing our full
potential. It's not about suppressing our creative energy—
far from it! It's about learning to channel it effectively, to
ground ourselves regularly so that we can continue to create and expand without burning out.

As we move forward, we'll explore practical techniques
for balancing this expansive energy with grounding practices. By mastering this interplay, you'll be able to tap into
your boundless creativity while maintaining a sense of

centeredness and calm.

Our Innate Superpower

At the core of our exploration lies a fundamental question: What does it truly mean to be a woman? This isn't just about societal roles or expectations. It's about understanding the very essence of feminine energy and its perfect expression. Imagine, if you will, a universal truth where everything becomes nothing, and then nothing becomes everything. This is the awakened state, the enlightened being that transcends all boundaries. It's both the end goal and the beginning, simultaneously everything and nothing. We can discuss this theoretically, but the real power lies in experiencing it.

While women and men share similar organs, there are crucial differences in how our brains function, largely due to the innate creative energy of the feminine. The female brain is a marvel of complexity and creativity. It's like a universe of interconnected thoughts, capable of processing multiple ideas simultaneously. This expansive thinking is the wellspring of our innovative power, but it can sometimes be overwhelming—even to ourselves! Think about those moments when you're deep in conversation with another woman. There's an energy that builds, a creative force that flows between you. Ideas spark and multiply, and conversations branch off in a dozen directions at once. It's exhilarating, isn't it? But to an outside observer, particularly a male one, it might seem chaotic or "too much."

This is because the male brain tends to prefer clarity

and precision. It's not that men aren't creative, but their thought processes often follow a more linear path. When faced with the whirlwind of feminine communication and creativity, they might feel overwhelmed or struggle to keep up. Understanding these differences isn't about reinforcing stereotypes or claiming superiority. It's about recognizing and celebrating the unique strengths of our feminine minds. Our ability to think creatively, to hold multiple ideas in tension, to see connections where others might not—these are superpowers.

As we move forward, we'll explore how to harness this creative energy effectively. We'll learn techniques to channel our expansive thinking when needed, and how to communicate our ideas clearly to those who might process information differently.

Remember, the goal isn't to change who we are or how we think. It's about embracing our natural gifts while developing the skills to navigate a world that doesn't always understand or appreciate the beautiful complexity of the feminine mind.

Why Self-Mastery is Different for Women

Imagine the universe as a grand dance of energies, with Mars and Venus leading the waltz. Venus, the goddess of beauty and love, embodies the essence of creativity and expansiveness. Mars, the god of war, represents force, direction, and penetrative energy. These celestial bodies mirror the interplay of masculine and feminine energies within each of us.

Now, let's journey into the fascinating landscape of our brains. The left hemisphere, often associated with masculine energy, is like a skilled architect. It's analytical, logical, and goal-oriented. It asks, "How do I get there?" and plots a direct course. This is the realm of structure, of breaking through barriers, of external achievement.

The right hemisphere, linked to feminine energy, is more like an abstract artist. It's intuitive, creative, and expansive. This is where we find the power of female intuition, that uncanny ability to "just know" without logical explanation. It's an internal force, endlessly expanding, seeking to understand through *being* rather than *doing*.

But here's the key: We all possess both energies, regardless of our gender, or where we see ourselves on the spectrum of gender. It's not about being a man or a woman. It's about the balance and interplay of these forces within us. Women often find their right brain energy is naturally stronger. This is why you might experience those moments of powerful intuition, or find yourself navigating complex emotional landscapes with ease. It's as if you're looking within, tapping into a vast internal universe. Men, on the other hand, may find their left brain energy more dominant. This manifests as a talent for strategy, for focusing and directing energy toward specific goals. It's like looking outward, mapping the external world with precision. Understanding these differences isn't about reinforcing stereotypes. It's about recognizing the unique strengths we each bring to the table. Women, your intuitive powers and ability to think creatively are not just "gut feelings," they're a manifestation of your brain's incredible capabilities.

As we move forward, we'll explore how to harness both energies effectively. For women, this might mean learning to channel your expansive, intuitive thinking into concrete action. For men, it could involve tapping into their intuitive side to complement their analytical strengths. The ultimate goal? To achieve a harmonious balance, where logic and intuition, structure and creativity, work in perfect synergy. This is the path to true awakening, where the illusions of self dissolve and we touch the essence of our being.

For us women, self-mastery requires a unique approach, one that acknowledges the beautiful intricacies of our minds and hearts. Understanding how our brains work differently from men's is crucial for every aspect of our lives, from relationships to career success. Remember that bestseller, *Men Are from Mars, Women Are from Venus*? Its core message still rings true: recognizing our differences is the key to harmony. I learned this the hard way in my relationship journeys. Like many of you, I've experienced deep connections, engagements, and even marriage, and watched them unravel because neither of us truly understood our fundamental differences.

But once you grasp these distinctions, relationships transform. Now, I can appreciate my husband on a whole new level, understanding that our thought processes and ways of experiencing the world are beautifully, necessarily different.

So, why is this understanding so critical? It's simple: Unmet expectations are the silent killers of relationships. Men often expect women to be direct and straightforward, while we expect men to be as intuitively connected as we are. Spoiler alert: That's not how it works!

In my years of relationship coaching, I've seen this scenario play out countless times: A woman is upset because she is expecting her partner to intuitively sense her feelings and respond accordingly. Meanwhile, her partner is waiting for her to clearly state what she needs. It's a dance of mismatched expectations that leads to frustration on both sides.

As women, we have this incredible ability to sense emotions, to feel the energy in a room. We can often tell when our friends, children, or partners are upset without a word being spoken. It's like we're tuned into an emotional frequency that men often can't access in the same way. But here's the crucial part: We can't expect men to operate on this same frequency. When we do, we're setting ourselves and our relationships up for disappointment. Similarly, when men expect us to communicate in their direct, linear style, they're missing out on the rich, nuanced way we express ourselves.

So, what's the solution? It starts with awareness. Recognize that your male partner's brain is wired differently. He's not being insensitive when he doesn't pick up on your subtle cues. He just genuinely might not see them. And when you need something, don't be afraid to express it clearly. It's not that he doesn't care. He's just not equipped to read your mind.

As we move forward, we'll explore practical strategies for bridging this communication gap. We'll learn how to honor our intuitive, expansive way of thinking while also developing skills to communicate effectively with the more linear male mind.

Unleashing Your Feminine Brain Power

Let's get fired up about the amazing potential of your female brain. While we often hear about the goal-oriented, competitive nature of the male mind, it's time to celebrate the unique superpowers of feminine cognition.

Your female brain is wired for connection, intuition, and holistic thinking. While men may pride themselves on developing sensitivity through practice, you've got an innate gift for emotional intelligence that's off the charts. It's not about being better. Rather, it's about embracing your natural strengths.

The masculine mind often operates like a laser beam—focused, direct, and always seeking to improve and achieve. But your feminine brain? It's more like a gorgeous, intricate web—sensing, feeling, and processing information from multiple angles simultaneously. This is your secret weapon in life and business.

When a man encounters a problem, his instinct is often to attack it head-on, to find the quickest route from A to B. But your feminine brain allows you to zoom out, to see patterns and possibilities that others miss. You're not just solving the problem—you're reimagining the entire landscape.

Now, I can already hear some of you saying, "But I want to be more focused and goal-oriented!" Here's the truth: You can absolutely cultivate those skills without dampening your feminine genius. The key is integration, not imitation. Imagine combining that incredible feminine intuition with razor-sharp focus. Picture harnessing your empathy and emotional awareness to become an unstoppable leader. That's the power of embracing your authentic feminine brain while strategically developing complementary masculine traits.

Let's break it down:

1. **Intuitive Decision-Making: Trust your gut!** Your female brain is processing vast amounts of subtle information. When you get that "feeling" about a situation or person, it's not magic. It's your super-computer at work.

2. **Relationship Mastery:** Your brain is built for connection. Use this to build unshakable networks, foster team synergy, and create loyal customers who feel truly seen and understood.

3. **Multitasking Maven:** While the jury's still out on whether multitasking is truly efficient, your female brain excels at juggling multiple streams of thought. Channel this into creative problem-solving and big-picture thinking.

4. **Emotional Intelligence:** Your capacity for empathy and reading social cues is a leadership superpower. Cultivate it to inspire and motivate others like never before.

5. **Stress Response:** The female brain has unique stress responses that can enhance social connection. Learn to leverage them for resilience and team-building in high-pressure situations.

Here are your action steps: I want you to keep a Brain Power Journal. Each day, note at least one instance where you leveraged a distinctly feminine cognitive strength. Maybe you defused a tense situation with your emotional awareness, or your intuition led you to an innovative solution.

Remember, it's not about denying the value of traditionally masculine traits. It's about recognizing that your female brain gives you an incredible foundation to build upon. By understanding and maximizing your innate cognitive gifts, while strategically developing complementary skills, you'll become an unstoppable force in both your personal and professional life.

Back to the men are from Mars and women from Venus question. Well, there's more truth to that than you might think. But the truth is, it's not about staying put on our home planets. It's about the journey between them. As women, we may start our journey on Venus. We're naturally tuned into that beautiful, expansive energy of love, creativity, and spirituality. It's our home base. But guess what? Our growth, our evolution, is all about learning to harness some of that Mars energy.

Now, I can hear some of you thinking, "I thought being feminine was enough!" True empowerment comes from integrating both energies. It's not about losing your femininity. It's about becoming a complete, unstoppable force of nature instead.

Now, here's where it gets really interesting. While we're on this journey toward Mars, guess what the guys are doing? They're on a spiritual quest toward Venus. They're learning to connect with their hearts, tap into intuition, and embrace the power of unconditional love. This cosmic dance creates some fascinating dynamics:

Safety vs. Love: Many women are drawn to men who make them feel secure in the material world (Hello, Mars energy!). Men, on the flip side, often stay with women who love them unconditionally (That's pure Venus).

The Integration Challenge: Just like some men never develop their spiritual side and become harsh or destructive, some women get stuck in their feminine energy without developing their ability to act and express themselves in the world.

Your Action Plan:

1. **Embrace Your Venus:** Celebrate your natural gifts of intuition, creativity, and connection. These are your superpowers.

2. **Mars Training:** Commit to developing your goal-setting, strategic thinking, and action-taking muscles. Start small, but start today.

3. **Express Yourself:** Find your voice and use it! Whether it's in your relationships, career, or

community, practice speaking your truth with confidence.

4. **Balance Check:** Regularly assess where you're at in your journey. Are you all Venus and no Mars? Time to level up your action game. Feeling disconnected from your feminine core? Schedule some nurturing, intuitive practices.

5. **Cosmic Appreciation:** Recognize and appreciate the journey that the men in your life are on too. Supporting each other's growth creates powerful partnerships and communities.

Remember, it's not about becoming less feminine. It's about becoming more whole. By embracing both your Venus essence and developing your Mars skills, you'll become an unstoppable force in this world.

Cultural Differences

It wouldn't be fair to all the women in the world not to take a moment to consider that in many parts of the world, women are still facing extreme suppression of their masculine energy. I'm talking about places where girls aren't allowed to go to school, can't leave the house until they're married, and are cut off from the system of the world. It's heartbreaking, and it's creating a crisis of empowerment and inequality.

But imbalance doesn't just happen in far-off places. It's happening right here, right now, maybe even to you. So let's break it down:

1. **The Suppressed Masculine:** When women are denied education, expression, and engagement with the world, their innate masculine energy gets locked down. This isn't just about career opportunities—it's about fundamental empowerment. Without this balance, women can become:

    - Disconnected from reality
    - Unable to strategize or plan
    - Vulnerable to manipulation and abuse
    - Financially dependent
    - Filled with unfocused, chaotic energy

Action Step: If you're feeling any of these symptoms, it's time to consciously develop your masculine side. Start small—take a class, learn about finances, and set and achieve a concrete goal.

2. **The Overpowering Masculine:** Now, flip the script. In many Western cultures, we've got women who are all masculine energy, all the time. They're crushing it in male-dominated fields, but at what cost? Here's what can happen:

    - Early menopause and hormonal issues
    - Burnout and exhaustion
    - Loss of intuition and creativity
    - Relationship struggles
    - A deep sense of disconnection

Action Step: If this sounds like you, it's time for some serious feminine reconnection. Schedule regular feminine energy time—meditate, do breathwork, and engage in creative pursuits without a goal.

3. The Sweet Spot of Balance: Here's the golden ticket: When you can dance between your feminine and masculine energies, you become an unstoppable force. You can:

- Navigate society with confidence
- Express yourself clearly and powerfully
- Maintain your health and vitality
- Access both intuition and logic
- Create success on your own terms

Action Step: Start a Balance Journal. Each day, note one action you took from your masculine energy and one way you honored your feminine essence. Watch the magic unfold.

Here's your challenge: For the next thirty days, commit to consciously developing your weaker energy. If you're all action and no intuition, schedule daily meditation. If you're all feelings and no structure, set and achieve one concrete goal each week.

The world needs empowered, balanced women now more than ever. We need your voices, your leadership, your unique blend of feminine wisdom and masculine action. True freedom comes when you can dance between the feminine and masculine within you. It's not about choosing one or the other. It's about embracing the fullness of who you are.

The Yin-Yang Dance: Mastering Your Energetic Balance

We're about to dive into the final piece of our energetic puzzle and trust me, this is where it all comes together. We're talking about the delicate dance between your feminine and masculine energies, and how getting it right can transform every aspect of your life.

Let's break it down:

1. **The Overcompensating Woman:** Have you ever felt like you're carrying the world on your shoulders? Maybe your partner isn't stepping up, or you're surrounded by conscious men who are more in touch with their feelings than their power. Here's what happens:

   • You push into overdrive with your masculine energy

   • Your menstrual cycle goes haywire

   • You're building empires but feeling disconnected

   Action Step: Check in with your body. Are you forcing yourself into constant action? It's time to consciously cultivate some yin to balance that yang!

2. The Energy Extremes:

Too Feminine:

- Dependency issues
- Lack of real-world skills
- Vulnerability to manipulation
- Financial struggles

Too Masculine:

- Early menopause
- Fertility challenges
- Relationship difficulties
- Disconnection from intuition

3. The Male Perspective:

Men face their own challenges:

Too Masculine:

- Aggression and insensitivity
- Destructive tendencies

Too Feminine:

- Lack of focus and discipline
- Prone to addictions
- Difficulty navigating the world

4. The Body Doesn't Lie:

Your physical form reflects your energetic state:

- Overly masculine women often have tension and stiffness

• Men drowning in feminine energy may
  seek escape through substance abuse

Your Balancing Act Challenge

1. Energy Audit: For one week, track when you're in masculine (action, planning) vs. feminine (intuition, receptivity) mode.

2. Conscious Cultivation: Each day, do one activity to nurture your less dominant energy.

3. Body Wisdom: Pay attention to physical signs of imbalance—tension, fatigue, menstrual issues.

4. Partner Check-In: If you're in a relationship, have an open conversation about energetic balance.

✦

We've now laid the groundwork for understanding your brain and energy. But knowledge alone isn't enough. It's time to put it into action.

Are you ready to take everything we've learned and transform it into unshakable personal power? Because we're about to dive into the five core principles of self-mastery, starting with the foundation of it all: breath work.

Why breath? Because it's the bridge between your conscious and unconscious mind, between your energy and your physical form. Mastering your breath is like grabbing the steering wheel of your entire being.

In the next section, we'll explore:

- The science behind breath work and its impact on your nervous system
- Powerful techniques to instantly shift your state
- How to use breath to balance your feminine and masculine energies
- Daily practices to increase your overall vitality and presence

Get ready to inhale power and exhale limitation. Your journey to true self-mastery starts with a single breath.

Sacred Reminders

✦ Your expansive, creative mind is a gift. While it may feel overwhelming at times, your ability to think holistically and hold multiple perspectives simultaneously is a feminine superpower.

✦ You are not meant to think or process information like a man. Your intuitive, non-linear way of understanding the world is valid and valuable.

✦ Balance is key. Use your masculine energy (30 percent) to ground and focus your expansive feminine energy (70 percent), not to override it. This creates harmony rather than internal conflict.

✦ Your intuitive knowing isn't just feelings. It's your brain processing vast amounts of subtle information in ways science is just beginning to understand.

✦ In relationships, remember that male and female brains operate differently. Don't expect men to intuitively sense what you need. Direct communication bridges the gap while honoring both ways of thinking.

✦ Your emotional intelligence and ability to sense subtle energies are not weaknesses. They are sophisticated cognitive strengths that enhance leadership, creativity, and problem-solving.

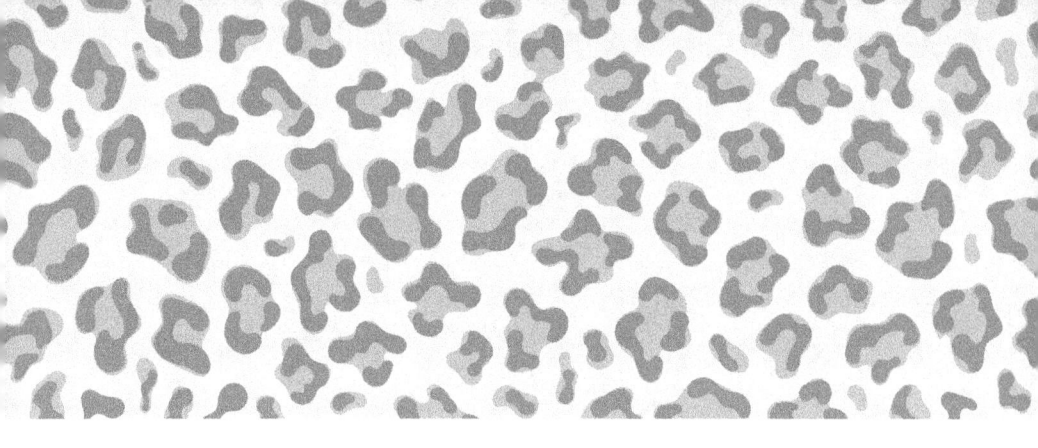

PART 2:

Self-Mastery Principles

Principle 1: Breath

Imagine a world where your every breath is a gateway to transformation and the simple act of inhaling and exhaling holds the power to revolutionize your life. This isn't a fantasy, but rather the extraordinary reality I've unearthed after years of intensive study and practice in the field of breathwork.

I've explored countless breathing techniques, trained experts worldwide, and ultimately developed a system I now call Transformal Breathing. This system is a distillation of the most effective methods I've encountered. Although there are a hundred methods and systems of breathing to try, the important thing to remember is that the most potent, life-altering breath of all is the one you were born with—your natural breath.

Natural breath is nothing short of miraculous. Throughout practices, training, and countless personal experiences, this fundamental truth has remained a constant. This is why I've set aside other techniques to focus solely on guiding people back to their innate breathing patterns.

Picture the pure, effortless breath of an infant. Our goal is not to learn something new, but to strip away years of accumulated tension and return to our most intrinsic state. When you begin to breathe naturally, you'll experience a profound shift and regain the transparency and natural-ness of a baby. This endless wellspring of purity will meet all your needs and allow you to experience life with an extraordinary absence of negative thought. Now this isn't about reverting to childhood. But rather infusing your adult self—your present age and body—with that same purity, transparency, and positive energy. When this happens, your life will transform swiftly and comprehensively.

These aren't utopian dreams. On the contrary, you're closer to this ideal state than you've ever been. By engag-ing with this book, you've taken a monumental step toward personal revolution. I've spent years helping people open their breath and have witnessed firsthand the splendid mir-acles it creates in their lives. Starting with my own journey, I've seen the power of breath work its magic thousands of times.

You're about to knock on a door that leads to extraor-dinary change. As you turn these pages, remember that the key to unlocking your full potential has been with you all along and waiting in the rhythm of your breath. Are you ready to harness this innate power and transform your life from the inside out? Let's embark on this breathtaking jour-ney together and unlock the miracles that await with every conscious inhale and exhale.

How Your Breath and Your Life Are Exactly the Same

In my book *Reflections*, I explore a profound truth that encapsulates the essence of our existence: "How we breathe is how we live." This isn't mere philosophy—it's a tangible reality I've witnessed countless times in breath sessions. Our breath is the mirror of our life, reflects our innermost states, and shapes our outer experiences.

Consider this: Every challenge and obstacle in your life is intrinsically linked to your breathing patterns. It's a startling revelation, yet undeniably true. We generate negativity—be it emotional turmoil, troubling thoughts, or physical ailments—by restricting our breath. To harbor illness, you must first hold your breath. Lies, fears, anxieties, and other negative states require a constrained breath to persist in your system.

Now, imagine the transformative power of Open and Connected Breath—a.k.a., the natural breathing state we're born with. When your breath flows freely, fatigue becomes a distant memory. Natural breathing restores us to our innate state of vitality and health. Open and connected breath isn't about gaining something new, but about reclaiming what's rightfully ours. Limited breathing habits trap negative emotions and thoughts within us. As we hold our breath, we inadvertently accumulate negative cellular energy. This, in turn, attracts more negativity into our lives and creates a self-perpetuating cycle.

Now that you're armed with this knowledge, you have the power to completely reverse this cycle. It's a universal law—change your breath, change your life. This is a consistent and observable phenomenon that occurs for everyone who embraces this practice.

Let me emphasize that the natural breathing techniques we explore are grounded in solid scientific principles. The transformation of your breath and mind isn't a matter of chance, but as certain as water boiling at 100 degrees Celsius. The outcome doesn't vary based on the volume of water or the material of the kettle. So, when you apply these techniques, you're guaranteed results. There's no risk and no uncertainty. As you continue to breathe freely and fully, you'll inevitably encounter your own miracles.

Are you ready to harness this transformative power and breathe your way into a life of boundless potential and vibrant well-being? The science is clear, the methods are proven, and the results are waiting. All that's left is for you to take that first, conscious breath toward a radically transformed life. Let's begin this breathtaking journey together and unlock the extraordinary power that resides within your every inhalation and exhalation.

Breath is Everything

After decades of intensive research, training, and hands-on experience with tens of thousands of individuals, I've arrived at a profound realization that natural breath is a blessing bestowed upon us. It surpasses all breathing trends, techniques, and methods in its sophistication and power.

My journey has led me through the entire spectrum of breathing practices on Earth. I've explored everything from yogic breathing and pranayama to holotropic and holistic approaches to chakra-opening and energy-balancing techniques to transformative breath and shamanic practices and nothing compares. Even the advanced transformative breath pales in comparison to the magnificence of natural breath.

The breath gifted to us by the Divine is a system that transcends all other techniques. It's a work of genius and a marvel of creation that outshines every method and system we've devised. As someone who has immersed herself in all breathing techniques for years and has been educated in their nuances, I urge you to release all learned breaths and embrace your natural breath. The specific awareness and potent light of natural breath are so profound that merely inviting it into your life will catalyze transformative change. This isn't just another technique—it's a consciousness and an inherent wisdom residing within you. Your only task is to intend and allow it to guide you.

When you align with your natural breath, you'll find yourself drawn to the right people, led down the most beneficial paths, and manifesting miracles in your life. Yes, I've created many miracles through holotropic and transformative breathing by applying specialized methods and exercises, but I've since discovered something even more powerful.

In the past, when I believed I could achieve anything, a nagging question always followed. "Is this truly right for me?" I would ask myself. "Is this the highest possibility for my life?" The answer was invariably, No. Why? Well, because no breathing technique or method, no matter how advanced, can fully unlock the experience you seek. On the other hand, natural breath has the power to manifest a life so perfect and complete that it surpasses even our wildest dreams. You'll witness this transformation when you liberate yourself from the perceived need for any technique, method, or system.

Breath and Positive Intention to Convert the Subconscious

As we delve deeper into the transformative power of breath, let's explore the intricate workings of the mind—a realm where our natural breath can create profound shifts.

Imagine your mind as a vast landscape with two distinct territories: the conscious and the subconscious. The conscious mind, like a well-lit stage, is easily influenced by affirmations and intentional thoughts. It's the realm where you can actively recognize negativity and consciously choose positivity. But, beneath this illuminated surface lies the subconscious—a deep, mysterious well of thoughts and patterns. This hidden realm, though less accessible, wields immense power over our lives. It's here that a single negative thought can attract challenging situations or people, which can often leave us wondering why we're surrounded by negativity.

Here's the revolutionary truth: The key to transforming this subconscious realm lies in the power of your natural breath. By opening and connecting your breath, you can initiate a perfect transformation, regardless of how deeply ingrained the negativity may be. And the potency of this transformation is astounding. When you master the art of reaching and maintaining a positive vibration through breath, your body becomes an impenetrable fortress. Even physical toxins are expelled effortlessly. At the first sign of illness, I will immerse myself in conscious breathing, and, within minutes, the symptoms dissipate. Despite an intensely demanding schedule, it's been a decade since I've succumbed to even a common cold.

But breath alone isn't the whole story. Positive intention plays a crucial role in this transformation. True positivity transcends material desires. It's not about visualizing a specific car or house as such concrete images can actually lower your vibrational frequency. Instead, focus on the essence of what you desire. Ask yourself, "How will I feel when I achieve this?" The answers—safety, renewal, and abundance—become your high-vibration intentions.

Remember, the mind perceives words individually, not in full sentences. "I don't want to fight," still puts the concept of fighting into your reality. Instead, affirm that "I want peace in all my relationships." You are the director of your life's movie so choose your words wisely and watch how dramatically the script changes.

As you embrace your natural breath and align with positive intentions, you'll notice a spontaneous shift in your choices and perceptions. Negativity will naturally fall away and will be replaced by an innate wisdom to guide you toward positivity in all aspects of life.

So, are you ready to harness this powerful combination of natural breath and positive intention to transform your deep subconscious? This journey begins with just a single, mindful breath. Let's embark on this extraordinary adventure together and unlock the full potential of your mind through the miraculous power of your natural breath.

Our Relationships

Fear is as natural to the human experience as breathing. It's hereditary, learned, and constantly reinforced through our experiences. Some of us boldly claim, "I'm not afraid of anything!" But, in doing so, we inadvertently reveal our deepest fear—the fear of being afraid.

My journey of understanding fear took a dramatic turn during a Landmark training in Amsterdam. I was in a room surrounded by ambitious individuals when I was suddenly confronted with the realization that deep fear resided within each of us. Initially, I resisted. How could I, a woman who traveled the world alone, be considered a coward?

But as the training progressed, a profound truth emerged. I accepted that we are all mysteries to each other as we each inhabit separate bodies and have thoughts and intentions hidden from view. So, how can we not be afraid when faced with such inherent uncertainty?

This realization might seem absurd at first. Imagine walking down a street and greeting a friend. The ridiculous but fundamental truth about human interaction is that you and your friend are secretly terrified of each other. This fear permeates all our romantic, professional, and familial relationships. We're constantly navigating the unknown and are uncertain of what the next moment might bring. Who knows if a loved one might suddenly change or if a stranger might become a lifelong friend? So, how do we live with this awareness? How do we build meaningful connections in the face of such uncertainty? The answer lies in a profound shift of focus. By acknowledging our fears and recognizing the impermanence of all external relationships, we can make the wise decision to invest our energy in the one relationship that remains constant: our relationship with ourselves.

This isn't about devaluing our connections with others, but recognizing that true security and peace come from within. Everything external will eventually change or end, but our inner self remains a constant presence. For the wise, solitude becomes a conscious choice, not a state to be avoided. It's an investment in a world of certainty and peace rather than expending energy in a realm of insecurity and fear. However, this path isn't easy, and it may be misunderstood by those who haven't made the same choice. But, for those who embark on this journey of self-mastery, it offers a profound sense of security and fulfillment.

Respiration

As we delve deeper into the transformative power of breath, let's explore the intricate relationship between our conscious breathing and the body's involuntary respiratory system. This understanding is crucial for harnessing the full potential of your natural breath.

For starters, breathing, in its essence, is a psychological

act. We have the remarkable ability to consciously alter our breath's rate, depth, and pattern. This is the foundation of various breathing techniques and the bridge between our conscious mind and our autonomic bodily functions.

Respiration, on the other hand, is a physical process governed by our brain stem. It's an involuntary reflex as automatic and essential as your heartbeat. Your brain, through millions of receptors scattered throughout your body, constantly gathers information about your internal state. It monitors pH levels, oxygen saturation, and countless other factors and adjusts your respiratory rate accordingly. This sophisticated system is designed for optimal function, yet many of us aren't utilizing our full lung capacity. Years of dysfunctional breathing habits can limit our respiratory potential and impact our overall well-being.

Paradoxically, even those who seem to have mastered breath control can fall prey to overbreathing. Consider professional opera singers who, despite their impressive lung capacity and diaphragm control, may experience onstage anxiety attacks or fainting. This phenomenon, known as hypocapnia, occurs when excessive use of the diaphragm leads to an imbalance in blood gases. Overbreathing, while less dramatic in everyday life, can still have significant impacts. Overbreathing is a condition well-documented in respiratory science where breathing too deeply or rapidly leads to a decrease in carbon dioxide levels in the blood, potentially triggering a range of physiological responses.

Understanding these nuances is crucial as we work toward optimizing our breath. The goal isn't to control every aspect of our breathing—that's neither possible nor desirable. Instead, we're aiming to cultivate awareness and harmony between our conscious breathing practices and our body's natural respiratory wisdom.

As you continue your journey with natural breath, pay attention to the subtle interplay between your intentional breathing and your body's automatic responses. Notice how different breathing patterns affect your physical and emotional state. Are there moments when you might be overbreathing without realizing it? How can you bring more balance and efficiency to your breath?

Our bodies function optimally at a slightly alkaline pH of 7.4. This precise balance is crucial for a myriad of bodily functions, but, perhaps most importantly, it's the ideal environment for our brain to operate at its peak capacity. When our pH is balanced, our cognitive functions are sharper, our emotional responses are more measured, and our overall sense of well-being is enhanced. Respiration plays a pivotal role in maintaining this delicate balance. With each breath, we're not just taking in oxygen, but participating in a complex biochemical dance that keeps our internal environment in perfect harmony. When our breathing is balanced and natural, it supports this optimal pH level and creates a physiological state that attracts positive thought patterns and emotional stability.

However, when our breathing habits become dysfunctional, it can lead to a cascade of effects that extend far beyond our lungs. Distorted breathing can disrupt pH balance and potentially distort thinking patterns. The connection between breath and mind is so profound that it can influence our mental health in ways we're only beginning to fully understand. Let me share a personal example that illustrates this powerful connection. My sister was diagnosed with bipolar disorder, a condition characterized by extreme mood swings and often managed with heavy medication. Intrigued by the potential impact of breath on her condition, we decided to analyze her breathing habits. What we discovered was remarkable. As we worked to balance her breathing patterns, aligning them more closely with her natural rhythm, we observed a corresponding balance in her symptoms. The extreme highs and lows began to level out and mirrored the newfound balance in her respiratory patterns.

This experience underscores the crucial truth that our breath is not just a biological function, but a powerful tool for psychological and emotional regulation. By returning to our natural breath, we're both optimizing our physical health and creating the ideal internal environment for mental and emotional well-being.

Meditation to Open Breath

The following exercise is for you to try at home on your own:

Find a comfortable seated position and close your eyes. Direct your attention to your breath and notice its natural rhythm without trying to change it.

As you inhale and exhale, allow each breath to deepen your relaxation. Notice as the tension in your body begins to dissipate.

Imagine a line extending from the base of your spine into the ground and let it provide a sense of stability and grounding.

Picture yourself near a calm body of water. Visualize dropping a pebble into its center and observe the ripples as they expand outward and gradually fade.

Now, apply this imagery to your body. Envision waves of relaxation spreading from your core outward. Let these waves flow through your chest, back, and along your spine. Feel the tension releasing from each muscle group as this sensation of relaxation moves down your body and through your abdomen, hips, legs, and feet.

Shift your focus to the space between your eyebrows and imagine a point of light here. In your mind's eye, watch this light extend outward beyond your immediate surroundings, beyond your city, and into the vastness of space.

From this mental vantage point, observe the Earth as a whole. Take in the landmasses, oceans, and atmosphere, and allow this broader perspective to provide a sense of calm and context to your current state.

Now, gradually bring your attention back to your immediate environment and become aware of the room around you.

Count down slowly from three to one.

Three: You're coming to the present time. More awake and refreshed.

Two: Stretch your body and feel the place under your foot.

One: Open your eyes.

Take a moment to note any insights or sensations you experienced during this exercise.

✦

This practice combines breath awareness with visualization techniques to promote relaxation and provide a broader perspective. By regularly engaging in this exercise, you can develop a greater capacity for stress reduction and self-awareness. The goal is to use your breath as a tool for achieving a calm, focused state of mind, which can be applied to various aspects of your daily life.

Sacred Reminders

✦ Your natural breath is a divine gift more powerful than any learned breathing technique. Trust that the breath you were born with holds the key to your transformation.

✦ How you breathe is how you live. Your breath patterns mirror your life patterns, so by liberating your breath, you liberate your entire being.

✦ Your breath is the bridge between body and spirit, conscious and unconscious mind. Through conscious breathing, you can access and transform even the deepest patterns.

✦ Negativity requires restricted breath to survive in your system. When you breathe freely and fully, you naturally release what no longer serves you.

✦ The relationship between breathing and respiration is delicate so don't force or over control your breath. Instead, allow its natural rhythm to guide you back to balance.

✦ Your breath has the power to restore your original state of vitality and health. You're not gaining something new through breathwork, you're just remembering what was always yours.

✦ When combined with positive intention, your natural breath becomes a powerful force for transforming your subconscious patterns and manifesting your highest possibilities.

Principle 2: Meditation

Meditation is a fundamental practice for self-mastery, think of it as your daily multi-vitamin for the soul. Its benefits extend beyond mere self-improvement, fostering a state of holistic health with minimal risk. Without regular meditation, you may find yourself mired in negative emotional states: anxiety, tension, restlessness, irritability, and a host of other debilitating feelings. These emotions can significantly hinder your personal growth and well-being.

The essence of meditation lies in turning inward and focusing your energy on the soul. This spiritual energy, being intangible, carries a higher positive charge than physical energy. By investing in this internal realm, you connect with your inner perfection, your core truth. This internal investment yields external dividends, positively influencing all aspects of your life.

Conversely, neglecting meditation results in an over-emphasis on the material world. Without balancing material pursuits with spiritual investment, your internal system can falter. The human body has a threshold for negativity. Exceeding this limit often leads to physical illness. Meditation serves as a crucial balancing mechanism to prevent this tipping point.

Thus, consistently turning inward through meditation will help you maintain equilibrium between your inner and outer worlds. This balance is essential for overall well-being and for maintaining alignment with your life purpose. That's why integrating meditation into your daily routine becomes a powerful tool for self-connection. It allows for more effective navigation of life's challenges.

Meditation can become more accessible through such practices as the "100 Happiness Breath," which helps overcome the common hurdle of transitioning from external chaos to internal calm. This approach minimizes the risk of unconscious resistance to meditation.

Start with fifteen to twenty minutes of breath-focused meditation daily, gradually increasing the duration, and over time you will see significant benefits. Ultimate truth is constant, unchanging, identical for everyone, and singular. True reality must meet these criteria, it cannot be fleeting or subject to change. This definition leads us to consider whether this describes a concept of God or a universal truth. Upon reflection, we realize that nothing in our observable world remains unchanged from birth to death. Even our perception of reality differs based on our perspectives. This raises the question: Is there anything that is truly beyond questioning? This line of inquiry challenges us to look beyond surface-level experiences and to seek a deeper understanding of existence. It encourages a more profound exploration of what we consider to be true and unchanging in a world of constant flux.

This line of inquiry leads us inward. When we look within, we find a constant presence. This inner reality embodies the qualities we associate with perfection: peace, love, power, and compassion. The ultimate truth we seek is not external but resides within us. Examining the world in this way and through this lens reveals the inherent uncertainty of external reality. At any moment, circumstances can change drastically, highlighting the underlying fear that permeates our material existence. As a result, by investing our energy in the external world, we inadvertently invest in this fear.

By engaging in meditation and contemplating these fundamental questions, we open ourselves to a broader perspective on life and our place within it. This practice not only enhances our daily experiences but also connects us to something larger than ourselves, potentially leading to greater clarity and purpose in our lives. This perspective doesn't advocate for complete detachment from the material world. Rather, it illuminates the importance of where we focus our energy. Those who choose to invest in their inner reality—in trust, love, and peace—naturally radiate these qualities outward. Conversely, neglecting this inner investment can lead to a life increasingly dominated by fear and insecurity.

The choice of where to invest our energy is ultimately personal. It's not about what we do externally, but where we direct our focus and resources internally. This decision shapes our experience of reality and our impact on the world around us. By recognizing the unchanging truth within ourselves and choosing to invest in our inner reality, we can cultivate a foundation of peace and security that remains stable amid life's uncertainties. This inner work becomes the cornerstone of true self-mastery, enabling us to navigate life's challenges with greater resilience and authenticity.

The Miracle Course

This is a course I have led many times over the years. The course aims to increase your internal cleansing or purification process and transform your main XX. One of the participants of the Miracle Course, Kirthi, said before she meditated: "I used to think about my children all the time. The kids will come home at this time and I have to cook until they come home, And I have to do this and I have to do that. I was constantly nervous." But after she began meditating, Kirthi noticed a change in her thoughts and demeanor: "I still cook, but because I do not think about my children constantly and I invest in myself, it's happening calmly and quietly. When I do it calmly and quietly, my inner understanding, happiness, and peace flow to both the food I cook and my children."

The fact is, every person who has completed the Miracle Course becomes a great transformation tool through their awareness. The joy, health, and wealth will increase for both the participant herself and the people around her. That's because your breathing opens you up for guidance, and gets you out of being lost in your daily life. You begin to make decisions by turning to your soul with spiritual wisdom instead. This occurs because as you invest in yourself, and integrate with the ultimate truth, your trust grows and you start to reflect that trust into the outer world. And when you concentrate on your soul, you start to become positive because the soul is much more positive than the material within, thus affecting your mental and physical positivity.

Consider Kirthi's experience again. Through meditation, she discovered a profound shift. While she still cooks and cares for her family, she now does so with a calm, centered presence. This inner peace flows into her actions, infusing both the food she prepares and her interactions with her children with positive energy. This transformation illustrates a crucial point: Even our loved ones, in the context of energy investment, can be considered "material." We have a choice to invest either in our inner selves—the source of our positivity—or in external concerns, which often breed negativity. Remember, the external world is inherently subject to change and uncertainty. By cultivating inner positivity, we can elevate not only ourselves but also those around us.

The impact of this inner work extends far beyond our immediate circle. An individual with an open breath can influence hundreds, even thousands of people. Those with exceptionally open breath might impact millions. This influence spreads like ripples in a pond, following the law of energetic pressure. As you meditate and invest in your inner self, you naturally affect your environment.

Participants who complete the Miracle Course become catalysts for transformation, enhancing joy, health, and abundance in their lives and the lives of those around them.

This open-breath state facilitates clearer guidance and decision-making. As a result, you begin to navigate life with spiritual wisdom and move away from being lost in daily minutiae. Likewise, as you invest in yourself and align with your inner truth, your self-trust grows, radiating outward. Focusing on your soul naturally increases positivity because spiritual energy is inherently more positive than material concerns. Ultimately, this shift positively impacts both your mental and physical well-being.

By choosing to invest in your inner self, you're not just improving your own life—you're creating a ripple effect of positive change that can transform your entire sphere of influence. This is the true power of self-mastery: It extends far beyond personal growth to touch and elevate the world around you.

After completing the Miracle Course, personal commitment becomes crucial. It's essential to carve out time for yourself, integrating these practices into your daily routine. Create a simple, effective plan: Decide when you'll perform your "100 Breaths" and morning exercises. Will you rise thirty minutes earlier, or find another dedicated time? Consider this carefully as transforming negative energies accumulated during sleep is most effective immediately upon waking. Delaying until noon risks allowing these energies to manifest as distress in your life. Prioritize morning hours for this transformative work when possible.

Incorporate a weekly breath session into your schedule. For added support and motivation, consider partnering with a fellow Miracle Course graduate. Consistency is key so make sure to aim for at least four to five consecutive weeks of uninterrupted practice. During these sessions, remember the power of intention. Each breath session opens your system, and without clear intent, you risk filling it with unfocused energy. Always set a clear intention to guide your practice.

The Miracle Course aims to deepen your internal cleansing, accelerate your purification process, and transform core traumas into positive energy. To maintain and enhance this transformation, immerse yourself in supportive reading material. The books suggested in this course are carefully chosen to attract positive information to your system.

Engaging in high-vibration exercises—from reading uplifting content to intentional positivity, affirmations, breathing, meditation, and physical exercise—keeps you operating at an elevated frequency. As a result, this consistent practice ensures that you become increasingly positive with each passing day.

But remember, this journey of self-mastery is ongoing. Your dedication to these practices is the key to unlocking lasting transformation. As I mentioned, by committing to this process, you're not just changing yourself; you're creating a ripple effect of positivity that can impact countless lives around you. Embrace this opportunity to elevate your life and, by extension, the world around you.

Meditation Techniques

We can categorize meditation methods into six main groups:

1. Techniques of Being

2. Techniques of Watching

3. Techniques of Intuitional Perception

4. Techniques of Thinking

5. Techniques of Focusing

6. Techniques of Connecting

Each meditation technique serves one of the five functions of the mind, whichever one needs to expand, to be refined, and to be enlightened.

1. Techniques of Being offer a profound pathway to heightened awareness, transcending the five primary functions of the mind to directly connect with our core existence. These cross-border techniques facilitate an experience of pure awareness, where all mental functions align and balance harmoniously.

This watching of the foundational function of the mind gives birth to intuitive perception. As we cultivate this watchfulness of our thinking mind from a place of pure existence, our inner awareness and intuition sharpen. This enhanced perception guides our actions, anticipates future events, and directs our focus with remarkable clarity. Thus, this watchfulness naturally evolves into the thinking function.

Our existence, now more acutely aware, processes intuitive messages, allowing us to concentrate on critical issues in our lives. Subsequently, the connecting function activates, enabling more effective interaction with our environment, problem-solving, and progress.

When grounded in existence and the state of being, these mental functions operate in synergy. The techniques aim to maintain this self-awareness not only during meditation but also in everyday, eyes-open experiences. This constant state of being facilitates the natural alignment and balance of our mental functions. Without this state of being, the mind struggles to connect with its natural state, often resulting in reactive behaviors and artificial stress. By practicing these techniques, we create a seamless integration between inner awareness and outer experiences, leading to a more balanced, intuitive, and effective approach to life.

Therefore, Techniques of Being serve as a powerful tool in the journey of self-mastery, offering a path to align mind, intuition, and actions with core existence. This alignment enables living from a place of greater awareness, balance, and authenticity, ultimately unlocking the mind's full potential for a more purposeful and effective life.

For those new to meditation, focusing solely on Techniques of Being is recommended. A consistent practice, ideally twice daily for at least a year, allows the state of being to expand. As this foundation solidifies, the ability to watch naturally emerges.

2. Techniques of Watching serve as powerful tools for developing acute awareness of our mental and physical states. These methods enhance our ability to observe without judgment, commentary, or attachment, offering a path to mental liberation. By cultivating this watchfulness, we free ourselves from the tyranny of ideas and incidents, maintaining presence in the moment and alignment with our essence. This practice unveils reductive thought patterns such as attack, criticism, and fear, providing insight into the sources of artificial stress in our lives.

While mindfulness techniques fall into this category, it's crucial to note that without a foundation in the state of being, these watching techniques can be challenging to implement effectively. Many who struggle with meditation often attempt watching techniques prematurely, leading to frustration and inconsistent practice. After mastering Techniques of Being, watching techniques can be practiced with eyes open or closed, with closed-eye methods serving as an ideal starting point. As proficiency grows, open-eye techniques can be introduced.

As watching expands, we develop an abstract awareness of emotions, thoughts, bodily activities, and events. This awareness becomes an intuitive guide, providing clear insight into appropriate actions, words, and behaviors. This guidance manifests as a deep knowing, accompanied by inner clarity and non-linear mental imagery. As a result, this process cultivates self-assurance, a state where certainty about one's path emerges without explicit reasoning. This intuitive wisdom becomes a powerful tool for navigating life's complexities with confidence and clarity.

By mastering these techniques, we unlock a higher level of self-awareness and intuitive guidance, essential components in the journey of self-mastery and personal growth.

3. Techniques of Intuitional Perception are advanced methods designed to expand wisdom within one's essential being. These techniques become accessible and effective when the practitioner has established a solid foundation in the states of being and watching. With these foundational states firmly in place, distinguishing between genuine intuitive perception and fear-based thoughts becomes significantly easier. This discernment is crucial, as those who attempt these techniques without proper preparation may mistakenly interpret ego-driven thoughts of fear, reaction, or criticism as intuition.

Regular meditation and functional breathing expand the states of being and watching, paving the way for living with intuitional clarity. Conversely, those who pursue mental elevation without deep meditative practice often confuse ego-based thoughts with intuition, leading to persistent problems. Overcoming surface-level, ego-driven thoughts requires depth in meditation—a process that demands time and consistent practice. There are no shortcuts in this journey, which is ultimately beneficial, ensuring that true intuitive perception is developed authentically.

Techniques of Intuitional Perception encompass methods for realizing creativity and dreams. However, it's crucial to approach these under the guidance of a credible meditation instructor. Without a proper foundation, attempts at creativity can yield negative outcomes when influenced by fear-based thinking.

As the state of watching expands, differentiating between intuitive thoughts and those related to the cyclical world becomes more natural. This clarity deepens intuitive relationships and unlocks creativity. Practitioners who persist with these techniques often find that opportunities align with their desires, knowing instinctively what actions to take at any given moment.

Together these advanced techniques, when properly mastered, can significantly ease life's challenges and facilitate the manifestation of your wishes. However, they require a strong foundation in the fundamental practices of being and watching, emphasizing the importance of a patient, structured approach to developing intuitive perception.

4. Techniques of Thinking are powerful tools designed to facilitate deep contemplation on specific issues. These methods often incorporate a sound or affirmation and can be used to explore ideas and experiences or uncover deeper meanings.

The primary objective of these thinking techniques is threefold:

- To liberate yourself from fear-based thoughts
- To recognize and cultivate authentic thoughts

- To establish a profound connection with
  creative information.

It's crucial to understand that without a solid foundation in the state of being, the mind's thinking function can
become overwhelmed during high-stress situations. This
overload can lead to the elimination of other mental functions, resulting in chaotic, uneasy, uncontrolled, and often
aggressive thought patterns. In the absence of a grounded
state of being, the mind becomes susceptible to an uncon-
trollable flood of ideas. At this point, attempting to calm
or stop the mind becomes extremely challenging, if not
impossible.

However, when the state of being is sufficiently expanded,
the thinking technique transforms into a formidable tool.
It's through this technique that many practitioners achieve
the life-changing experience of "I got everything I wanted."
This realization marks a profound moment of understanding and alignment with your deepest desires and intentions.

The power of these thinking techniques lies in their ability to harness and direct the mind's natural tendency to
analyze and explore. When properly employed, they can
lead to breakthroughs in personal growth, problem-solving,
and creative endeavors.

To effectively utilize these techniques:

- Establish a strong foundation in the state
  of being through consistent meditation
  practice
- Choose a specific issue or idea to focus on

- Use a chosen sound or affirmation as an anchor for your thoughts
- Allow your mind to explore deeply, free from fear-based limitations
- Remain open to insights and creative information that may arise

5. Techniques of Focusing are advanced methods designed to cultivate unwavering attention on a specific object or idea. These techniques require a strong foundation in the states of being, watching, intuitional perception, and thinking to be effectively utilized.

Historically, these practices were employed by monastic practitioners for extended periods, serving as a means to stabilize a mind overwhelmed with thoughts. However, it's crucial to master the other mental functions before attempting these advanced focusing techniques. Many people, in their eagerness to progress, mistakenly believe that learning multiple meditation techniques simultaneously is beneficial. This approach, however, is counterproductive. Meditation is not a buffet where you can sample various techniques at will. Mastery of foundational practices is essential before advancing to more complex methods.

The power of meditation lies not in the quantity of techniques known, but in the depth of practice in a single, well-suited method. This principle of less is more applies not only to meditation but to many aspects of life. Consider your possessions, your knowledge, and your activities. Now how much of what you accumulate truly serves a purpose or brings value to your life?

In today's world, there's a tendency to pursue breadth at the expense of depth. People often seek to know a little about many things rather than gaining a profound understanding of one area. However, true mastery and its benefits come from deep engagement with a single practice or subject.

For those eager to explore the vast landscape of meditation and breathing techniques, resources abound in our modern world. Yet this abundance can be deceiving. Without a proper foundation, self-guided exploration often leads to scattered practice and superficial understanding. It's like trying to build a skyscraper without first laying a solid foundation—the structure may rise quickly, but it won't stand the test of time.

The most powerful approach is to choose one technique and dive deep, like a well digger who knows that one deep well yields more water than several shallow ones. This principle of mastery through depth rather than breadth extends beyond meditation into all areas of life. Just as a master musician must first perfect their scales before attempting complex compositions, a meditation practitioner must establish strong foundational practices before venturing into advanced techniques.

Quality of practice matters far more than the number of techniques you know. Think of it as tending a garden. As you may know, it's better to nurture one healthy plant to full bloom than to scatter seeds everywhere hoping something will grow. Likewise, as you develop depth in your practice, you'll find that understanding flows naturally like water finding its way through fertile soil.

Through consistent, focused practice of a single technique, you'll develop a meditation practice that transforms not just your spiritual life but every aspect of your being. This transformative power comes not from collecting techniques like trophies, but from the patient, persistent cultivation of deep understanding. True meditation emerges from this dedicated focus, blooming like a lotus flower from the depths of still waters.

6. Techniques of Connecting represent the pinnacle of meditative practice, aligning all five functions of the mind with the state of being to achieve harmonious operation. These powerful methods integrate all mental functions to connect with a desired focal point. Due to their advanced nature, these techniques are typically recommended only after a year of consistent meditation practice.

These connecting techniques are versatile, allowing practitioners to forge deep connections with various aspects of their experience, including breathing, emotions, thoughts, feelings, and surroundings. One particularly powerful application involves two individuals connecting heart-to-heart while maintaining eye contact, though variations can be practiced with eyes closed as well.

It's crucial to understand that meditation is universally accessible. We are all connected to one consciousness, and with proper guidance and methodology, anyone can develop a meaningful meditation practice. However, without self-awareness and remaining present, focused, and calm, it can be challenging. This is because the harmonious operation of the mind's five functions requires a deep foundation in the state of being and enhanced self-awareness.

The State of Being Meditation Technique outlined in this book serves as an excellent starting point. For those who find it challenging to maintain a daily practice of twenty minutes morning and evening, seeking guidance through structured classes can be beneficial. Consistent, disciplined practice over several years can prepare you for more advanced techniques.

As we conclude this exploration of meditation techniques, it's important to recognize that your journey in meditation is uniquely yours. To fully embrace this path, commit yourself to daily practice and make it as integral to your routine as eating or sleeping. This consistency is the bedrock of progress.

When you encounter challenges or feel uncertain, don't hesitate to seek guidance. A knowledgeable instructor or supportive community can provide invaluable insights and encouragement. Remember, even the most accomplished meditators once began as novices. Patience is crucial on this journey. Progress in meditation often occurs subtly, and breakthroughs may come when least expected. Trust in the process and remain steadfast in your practice, even when immediate results aren't apparent.

As you advance, remain open to deepening your practice. What begins as a simple daily ritual can evolve into a profound tool for self-discovery and transformation. Be receptive to new techniques and experiences as they present themselves.

While the structure and guidance provided here are valuable, they are merely signposts on your path. Your commitment and consistency are the true catalysts for change. As you persist in your practice, you'll uncover new layers of self-awareness and connection. These discoveries will not only enrich your meditation experience but will also ripple outward, fostering profound personal growth and a deep sense of inner harmony.

Embrace this journey with an open heart and a dedicated spirit. The transformative power of meditation awaits, ready to unveil the depths of your being and illuminate the path to your highest self.

Sacred Reminders

✦ Meditation is not just self-improvement. It's your daily soul nourishment, creating harmony between your inner and outer worlds.

✦ Without regular meditation, negative emotions accumulate and block your growth. By turning inward daily, you maintain the delicate balance required for well-being.

✦ Your spiritual energy carries a higher positive charge than physical energy. When you invest in your inner realm through meditation, you connect with your core truth and perfect nature.

✦ The unchanging truth you seek resides within you. While the external world constantly shifts, your inner presence remains constant and reliable.

✦ There are many meditation paths but mastery comes through depth rather than variety. Focus on one technique that resonates with you until it becomes natural.

✦ Remember that each stage of meditation builds upon the last. Begin with being before watching, watching before intuiting, always honoring the natural progression of awareness.

✦ Your commitment to regular practice is the key that unlocks lasting transformation. When you dedicate time to meditation, you're not just changing yourself—you're creating ripples of positive change that touch countless lives.

Principle 3: Mind

Your thoughts are incredibly powerful, even though they don't have physical form. That's because they're the starting point for everything you create in your life.

Think about getting sick. You might believe you caught a cold because you were in a draft. But it's your belief that drafts cause colds that leads to illness, not the draft itself. That's because everything begins in your mind. When you decide to put a book on a shelf, your thought sends a message to your body to take action. This same process applies to how you look and feel. Nothing happens in the physical world first. Everything starts in the thought dimension and then appears in our physical reality.

This means that if you want to change something in your life, focusing only on the physical level isn't effective. For example, if you want to lose weight, diet and exercise alone aren't enough. You need to start with your thoughts. This principle applies to all aspects of life—health, relationships, and success. Your mind has immense creative power. The key is to align your thoughts with positive, high-vibration energy.

Your mind is the control center of your life. When you learn to master your thoughts, you can create the reality you want. It's time to use this power to shape your life in meaningful ways.

Japanese scientist Masaru Emoto conducted an interesting study called the Water Crystals Experiment. He froze water from a pond and directed different thoughts toward it. When he examined the water under a microscope, he observed striking results.

When Emoto sent negative, angry messages to the water, the frozen crystals formed irregular shapes.

When he exposed the water to metal music, the crystals took on a different form.

However, when Emoto directed warm, positive messages to the water, the crystals formed beautiful, symmetrical patterns.

Many scientists have repeated Emoto's experiment since then. The results have been consistent enough to be considered a scientific principle. Many books about the power of thought reference this experiment. It demonstrates how thoughts can affect physical matter, including our bodies and our lives.

✦

In our breathing sessions, we use practices inspired by Emoto's work with water. As you practice these breathing techniques, you reach a higher vibrational state. At the same time, you receive new mental codes that can refresh your entire being, even your outward appearance.

Breath and Positive Intention

The mind has two main parts: the conscious mind and the subconscious mind. The conscious mind is easier to change. You can use affirmations to transform it because you're aware of your thoughts. When you notice a negative thought, you can consciously change it to a positive one.

The subconscious mind is more complex. If the conscious mind has fifty units of power, the subconscious has thirty. It's like a deep, dark well. You don't know what's in there or what you don't know about it. In this way, a negative thought in your subconscious can attract difficult people into your life. You might think these people are negative, but they're just playing a role. They could be very positive in general, but they act negatively toward you because of the law of attraction.

Thankfully, transforming the subconscious is possible through proper breathing techniques. When you learn to reach and maintain a positive vibration, your body becomes incredibly resilient. Even if you encounter something harmful, your body can reject it. Breathing techniques and positive intentions are crucial for transforming the subconscious mind. The more positive your intention, the higher the vibration you can reach.

Now let's explore what positive really means. Specific material desires, like a house with pink shutters or a red Ferrari, aren't truly positive. That's because they're too specific and tied to the physical world. As a result, this kind of thinking keeps you in a lower vibration. That's why focusing on such specific material items is sometimes called a curse in spiritual teachings. It can pull your energy down.

Instead of thinking, "I want black shoes," ask yourself, "How will I feel when I buy black shoes?" Look for broader, less material answers. When you do this, you might realize you're seeking a feeling of newness rather than just new black shoes. So, make that your intention instead. Another example: How will you feel when you own a house? If you think you'll feel safe, then make safety your intention. The less tied to physical things your intention is, the closer it is to creative vibration. This makes it more positive.

So, instead of focusing on a red Ferrari, set your intention on wealth. Or aim for feelings like fullness, gentleness, or success.

I've experienced this personally. When I feel a virus in my body, I use my breathing techniques. Within fifteen minutes, the illness is gone. I haven't had a cold in ten years, even though I work very hard. But that's because I can keep going when others get tired thanks to my breath work.

Understanding how the mind processes positives is crucial. The mind interprets words individually, not in complete sentences. For example, saying "I don't want to fight with my friends" isn't a positive intention. Your mind focuses on the word "fight," potentially bringing conflict into your life. Instead, say "I want to be at peace with everyone" to invite peace.

Another example, when you call someone or yourself stupid, you're inviting that quality into your life. I experienced this recently. Just three minutes after saying, "One man can't be that stupid," I made a foolish mistake myself. Similarly, calling someone a liar might lead you or others to lie more often. Remember, you're the director of your life. Replace negative words with positive ones. You'll be amazed at how much your life changes.

As you practice proper breathing techniques, finding positives becomes easier. Your system naturally rises to a higher level. You'll stop using words that distance you from positivity. You might find yourself doing something else during the news hour or choosing to watch comedies when you turn on the TV. These changes happen spontaneously. Essentially, as you become more positive, your reality changes to match. Life becomes more positive when you are positive. Your inner wisdom guides you toward better choices and experiences.

The Science

Albert Einstein described the electromagnetic field as the most basic element of physical reality. For a long time, scientists thought quantum effects only happened with tiny particles. But in the last ten years, they've seen these effects in bigger things, even in living creatures.

Quantum mechanics, sometimes called quantum entanglement, isn't just about small particles anymore. Scientists have now proven that quantum behavior happens on a larger scale. It might apply to everything, possibly even people. As a result, your mind and thinking habits can change the frequency of energy around you. That's because the universe of light energy is always there, but your mind connects with different parts of it. Ultimately it is this connection that shapes your reality.

Overall, only your mind's frequency and how you manage your thoughts can change. This is why some people live in a world of constant change, while others feel stuck in cycles of gaining and losing. But in reality, nothing is truly gained or lost. When you learn something new, you also forget something old. The total amount of possibilities always stays the same. Even the early universe, when it was tiny, had the same number of possible states as it does now. We think things are evolving and changing, that we're gaining or losing, but actually, nothing is really changing. According to quantum mechanics, the total number of possible states in a system never changes.

Things seem to change because systems naturally move toward their most common state, like how temperature and pressure balance out. Likewise, your thoughts can be orderly, balanced, grateful, and loving, or they can be messy, unbalanced, ungrateful, and emotional. It is the relationship between these different types of thoughts that is what's important. Understanding this can help you manage your mind better and create the reality you want.

Things to Watch Out For

When you catch yourself saying, "One day" or "I'll do it after," pause and reflect. These phrases are warning signs that you're deferring important actions in your life. By postponing meaningful engagement, you risk becoming a mere spectator in the stadium of your own existence, watching life unfold without actively participating. Ask yourself instead, "What am I waiting for?" Remember, time is finite, and continually putting things off can lead to regret.

To begin developing this self-awareness, I want you to actively document your thoughts. This exercise will give you a tangible record of your inner dialogue. Whether you are having a great day or a bad one, consistently writing down thoughts and feelings can be powerful when done consistently. This comprehensive approach will encourage an honest self-assessment. Next, analyze how these thoughts affect you emotionally. This crucial step will help you understand your mental landscape better. You'll start to recognize which thought patterns benefit you and which are detrimental to your well-being.

Here's an example of the transformation. Let's say there is someone called Allison in your life and every day Allison does something that annoys you. Why does Allison do this? The answer is in the law of attraction, which is one of the constant laws of life. The law of attraction works in many ways, both in tandem with positive and negative emotions and energies equally. If Allison is annoying you so much, take a step back and notice how you react to her actions or her words. Are you engaging with her energy at the same level that she is spewing it out into the world, which in this case would be a lower negative level? Or are you present-minded and engaging in a way that is more empathetic and kind, understanding that her negative emotions may not be due to anything that you have done but something that she is going through? When situations that involve negative emotions and energies are met with a present mind and openness it defuses the flames and makes the situations much less harmful to the one receiving the negativity. The positive law of attraction is at work once you can get yourself into this state of mind.

Here's the thing, all thoughts are open to questioning. This challenges the idea that any of your beliefs are absolutely certain. Embrace intellectual humility and be open to new perspectives. When you wonder which thought is right, consider that life itself, rather than any particular thought, is the ultimate arbiter of truth. By following these steps, you'll embark on a journey of self-discovery and mental clarity. This process will help you navigate your thoughts more effectively while also giving you the tools to not be as harmed by other people's negativity.

As you navigate through life, you'll often find yourself faced with a choice: to understand life or to experience it. Think of it like a football game. Are you on the field, actively playing, or are you sitting in the stands, watching and analyzing? You might feel an urge to constantly analyze and understand every aspect of your life. However, I want you to consider that you can't truly experience life while you're busy trying to understand it. When you're caught up in analysis or criticism, you're distancing yourself from the immediacy of your experiences.

When you actively participate in life, you're likely to feel healthier, more vital, youthful, and balanced. On the other hand, if you're always observing from the sidelines, you might find yourself feeling stagnant, bored, and discontent.

Consider how these different approaches might be impacting your own life right now. I'm not suggesting that you need to be actively engaged every single moment. Just as football players need to rest, you too need periods of reflection and inaction. These are natural and necessary. What's important is your mindset during these rest periods. Are you like a player, resting to get back in the game? Or are you a perpetual observer, criticizing without any intention to engage?

Play the Game of Life

For as long as I have been doing group work sessions I have almost always, without fail, been asked the question, What should I do? This is an example of being in the stands when you need to be out on the field. Rather than taking the initiative, people who ask this question are looking for external direction from a source that they seem to trust more than themselves. The role of a mentor or guide is, more or less there to facilitate clarity along with decision-making and personal empowerment. However, a mentor is not there to provide specific instructions. The emphasis on personal responsibility is paramount. Only you, the individual, can enter the game and play in your own life. This stance challenges the tendency to look to others—be it mentors, family members, or peers—for solutions to personal challenges.

It's crucial that you recognize your power to shape your life experiences and outcomes. This isn't about someone else making decisions for you. It's about you taking charge of your journey. I'm inviting you to make a conscious decision about your role in life. Will you be a player or a spectator? This isn't a rhetorical question. It's a call for you to reflect on your level of engagement with your life and choose deliberately.

Now that I have hammered that into your psyche, let's talk more about meditation. It's a powerful tool for self-understanding and managing anxiety. When I suggest opening windows to your worries, I'm not asking you to dwell on them, but rather to examine them without avoidance. This process can help you deal with your concerns more effectively. You might find, as many do, that distracting thoughts persist during meditation. This is entirely normal, whether you're a beginner or an experienced practitioner. When you try to quiet your mind and find it becoming more active instead, don't see this as a failure. It's a natural part of the process. Think of your thoughts as moving energies that are seeking expression. When you attempt to suppress or ignore them, you're essentially transforming what could be positive, fluid energy into negative, static energy. This isn't just theory; psychological research supports the idea that thought suppression can be counterproductive.

I want to propose a shift in how you view these thoughts. Instead of seeing them as distractions to be eliminated, try viewing them as your mind's attempts to communicate important information to you. This perspective invites you to approach your mental activity with more acceptance and curiosity. By doing so, you might discover insights about yourself that you hadn't considered before.

There is a level of importance that comes with meditation

for our minds, bodies, and our quality of life. Unaddressed thoughts can accumulate and transform into anxieties. Imagine leaving your child with a friend. If you give clear instructions to your friend about when nap time is, what his favorite stuffed animal is, and so on, you are taking action. If you don't take action, those questions may arise within your friend and anxieties may rise within your child. The idea is that when we take action and cover our bases, we can rest assured that the anxieties or worries we may have had due to suppressed thoughts and feelings will no longer be present.

Here's the thing, your persistent anxiety or fear isn't a single, monolithic entity. It's more likely the result of numerous positive thoughts that you've ignored over time. This might sound counterintuitive, but anxiety can be a symptom of neglected mental processes rather than an inherent state of being. What I'm suggesting is that what you perceive as negative emotions oftentimes has roots in unexpressed or uninitiated positive impulses. This challenges the common view of anxiety as purely negative. Instead, try to see it as a signal of unexplored potential.

But if you're experiencing anxiety, it may also indicate that you haven't expressed your thoughts or acted on them for a long time. This puts the responsibility for your emotional well-being in your hands. Anxiety isn't something that just happens to you. Rather, it's often the result of long-term patterns of thought suppression or inaction. By framing anxiety as the real face of your worries, I'm inviting you to see it not as an insurmountable emotional state, but as the understandable result of specific mental habits. This perspective can help you approach your anxiety with more understanding and less fear.

I encourage you to take this proactive approach to your mental health. By addressing your thoughts as they arise and taking appropriate action, you can prevent anxiety from building up over time. Going forward, try to view your thoughts not as burdens to be managed, but as valuable signals guiding you toward necessary actions or expressions. This shift in perspective can empower you to take charge.

Oftentimes, people tend to hold onto things in life for longer than might be healthy. Think about an old bag you've had for twenty years. You might keep it even though it's worn out and not very useful anymore. Your thoughts and emotions can be like this bag. You hold onto them because they're familiar, even if they're no longer serving you well. It can be challenging to let go of these long-held beliefs or emotional states, even when you know intellectually that they're outdated or even harmful because in some ways they're comforting to you. They're what you know.

Take Pause

Take a moment to reflect on your thoughts, beliefs, and emotional patterns. Are there any that you're clinging to simply because they're familiar? Just as you might benefit from updating your physical possessions, you might find it helpful to refresh your mental and emotional landscape. You might notice that you identify strongly with certain depressed thoughts, energies, or reactions. This is similar to how you might feel attached to old possessions. Even as you desire change, positivity, and innovation in your life, you might find yourself holding onto long-established thought patterns and fears. Many of us have internalized these patterns to the point where we see them as an integral part of who we are.

The more easily energy flows through you, the more positive you become. On the flip side, when you resist change, you invite negativity, rigidity, and even poor health into your life. However, when you are open to change it can completely flip your entire life around in a very positive way. And when these internalized thoughts and feelings are brought to light and dealt with you create a beautiful canvas for life.

You might define yourself with statements like "I am always principled" or "I have unbreakable rules." While these might seem like positive traits, they can block your energy flow. That's because you're identifying with thoughts and emotions that may not truly represent your essence, and this can hinder your natural positivity. It's easy to think that surrounding yourself with positive people will automatically make your life peaceful and cheerful. But that's not the whole story. True positivity requires you to transform yourself and take risks. It means challenging your long-held identities and fears, trying new experiences, and being open to the possibility of failure. You might notice a paradox between maintaining a fixed character and being truly positive. Your identity, your insistence on being a certain way, is often at the root of your problems. This is what we call the ego.

This understanding can help explain many health issues and societal problems. If you're part of a society that prides itself on being rock solid, you might be lacking the necessary flow and movement for true positivity and well-being. If you're dreaming of a more positive world or wishing others would change, remember that it starts with you. Your personal transformation is the first step toward positivity, and this individual change can ripple out to affect the entire world around you.

At the core of life, there's a simple formula: What you give is what you receive. You'll notice this, especially in your relationships, which often mirror your true personality. Your self-perception might not always match reality. The thoughts you have about yourself don't necessarily define who you are. When you truly understand and accept this, it can lead to profound changes in your life. Think of your relationships as mirrors. They reveal your authentic self, regardless of how you describe yourself. Whether you think you're generous or stingy, it's your interactions with others that ultimately shape how you're perceived. Every moment gives you a chance to reinvent yourself. Your behaviors and conversations define you more than your internal thoughts. By changing these external expressions, you can alter not only how others see you but also who you fundamentally are.

Remember, though, that real change requires action. Simply wishing for transformation without changing your behavior won't get you far. Mind Yoga offers tools for this mental transformation. Instead of trying to control your thoughts, it focuses on recognizing, understanding, accepting, and forgiving them. These steps are crucial for any lasting change.

To truly let go of something, whether it's a thought pattern, a behavior, or part of your identity, you first need to acknowledge its existence. Then, try to understand where it comes from and how it impacts your life. And then finally, accept its role, and forgive yourself or others associated with it. This process of self-examination and conscious change aligns with the idea of positivity as flow and adaptability. By embracing these principles, you open yourself to continuous growth and transformation, moving closer to your authentic self and overall well-being.

Sacred Reminders

✦ Everything in your physical reality begins as a thought. Your mind is the fertile soil from which your entire life grows, tend it with conscious awareness and positive intention.

✦ Your subconscious mind holds immense creative power. Through proper breathing and elevated thinking, you can transform even your deepest patterns and manifest profound change.

✦ True positivity transcends material desires. Instead of focusing on specific objects or outcomes, connect with the feelings you seek— peace, abundance, and renewal. These higher vibrations manifest more readily than concrete wishes.

✦ Choose your words with care as they program your reality. The mind processes each word individually, so speak and think in terms of what you want to create, not what you wish to avoid.

✦ Be a player, not a spectator, in your own life. True transformation requires active participation, not just observation. Your power lies in conscious engagement with life, not analysis from the sidelines.

Principle 4: Purpose

Understanding your true self and aligning with your purpose is a fundamental part of your personal growth and fulfillment. This journey of self-discovery involves peeling back layers of societal expectations, learned behaviors, and limitations you've imposed on yourself to reveal the authentic core of who you are. Your process begins with introspection—taking a deep dive into your thoughts, feelings, values, and experiences. This self-examination often requires you to confront uncomfortable truths and challenge long-held beliefs about yourself and the world. Ask yourself probing questions: What truly motivates you? What are your deepest values? What brings you genuine joy and satisfaction?

As you gain clarity about your authentic self, your next step is to align this understanding with your sense of purpose. Remember, your purpose doesn't have to be a grand, world-changing mission. It can be as simple as living in harmony with your values or using your unique gifts to contribute positively to the world. This alignment might involve making difficult choices. You may need to let go of pursuits that no longer serve you or take risks to follow a path that resonates more deeply with your core identity. It's about creating a life that feels authentic and meaningful to you, rather than one that just meets external expectations.

Keep in mind that this journey of self-discovery and purpose alignment is ongoing. As you grow and evolve, your understanding of yourself will deepen, and your sense of purpose may shift. This requires a commitment to continuous self-reflection and a willingness to adapt and change course when necessary.

Living in alignment with your true self and your purpose taps into a wellspring of energy, creativity, and satisfaction that enriches not only your own life but also the lives of those around you. It provides you with a sense of direction and meaning, enhances your decision-making, and fosters resilience in the face of life's challenges.

What is Purpose?

Discovering your purpose is like finding your personal North Star, the guiding light that gives your life direction and meaning. Your purpose isn't some lofty, unattainable ideal. It's deeply personal and as unique as your fingerprint. Think of it as your special way of contributing to the world. Your impact doesn't have to be Earth-shattering. Maybe your purpose is to bring joy through your cooking or to nurture young minds as a teacher. What matters is that it resonates with your true self.

But beware: Don't fall into the trap of thinking your purpose is set in stone. As you grow and change, your sense of purpose might shift too. That's not only okay, it's natural. Life is a journey of discovery, after all. The key is to keep checking in with yourself to make sure your actions still align with what feels meaningful to you.

Now, finding your purpose isn't always easy. It requires quite a bit of soul-searching. But you can begin by asking yourself: What activities make you lose track of time? What issues get your blood pumping? What kind of legacy do you want to leave? These questions can help point you in the right direction.

Despite what you might see on social media, living with purpose doesn't mean every moment needs to be filled with grand gestures. It's about bringing intention to your daily life and making choices that reflect your values. It's about finding meaning in both the big moments and the small ones. When you're aligned with your purpose, you'll find it easier to make decisions like these. That's because you develop a sort of internal compass that helps you navigate life's challenges. And when times get tough, your sense of purpose can equip you with a powerful source of resilience.

Remember, your purpose can change over time. The goals and aspirations that drove you in your twenties might look quite different from what motivates you in your forties or fifties. This evolution is perfectly normal, in fact, it's a sign of growth. As you accumulate experiences, gain new perspectives, and face different life stages, your understanding of what gives your life meaning can change. Embracing this changeability allows you to remain open to new possibilities and prevents you from feeling stuck in outdated notions of who you are or what you should be doing. Regularly check in with yourself by asking: Does this still resonate with me? Am I still fulfilled by this path?

Women Get Conditioned

As a woman, you've likely experienced a more pervasive form of societal conditioning than men. This conditioning, rooted in complex cultural, historical, and social factors, shapes your behaviors, beliefs, and self-perceptions in ways that can be subtle and challenging to recognize. From your early childhood, you've been subjected to messages about how you should behave, appear, and aspire. While often well-intentioned, these directives can create deep-seated beliefs that may not align with your authentic self. You might have internalized phrases like "Be nice," "Don't be too assertive," or "Prioritize others," which can influence your decisions and behaviors even now.

Addressing this conditioning is crucial for connect-ing with your authentic self. It requires you to consciously unlearn and reexamine your ingrained beliefs. This journey begins with self-awareness—recognizing how this condi-tioning influences your thoughts and actions. You can start by questioning your long-held beliefs. For example, when you face self-limiting thoughts or hesitations, ask yourself: Is this truly my own belief, or is it a product of societal expec-tations? Your intuition can be a powerful tool here. Often, your authentic self communicates through gut feelings or instincts that may contradict your learned behaviors. Pay attention to these internal signals as they can guide you toward more genuine choices.

Exposing yourself to diverse perspectives can also help you recognize and challenge your conditioning. Encountering varied viewpoints can illuminate how many societal norms and expectations are constructed, not inherent truths. But remember, this process of deconditioning isn't about rejecting everything you've learned. Rather, it's about consciously selecting which elements align with your true self and discarding those that don't serve your personal growth and authenticity.

This journey of connecting with yourself is ongoing and requires patience, self-compassion, and a willingness to embrace discomfort. The reward, however, is significant: A life lived with greater authenticity, where your choices stem from your genuine desires and values rather than ingrained responses.

Applying Purpose

Your journey to find purpose is deeply connected to your desires for growth, fulfillment, and authenticity. As you navigate life's transitions, seeking new experiences while dealing with the comfort of the familiar, you might often find yourself at a crossroads. In my work with many different people—from artists to doctors, managers to housewives—I've noticed a common thread: Everyone is searching for health, balance, happiness, peace, and security. This universal quest is, at its core, a pursuit of purpose.

Your mind has an inherent wisdom that, when listened to, can guide you toward your authentic purpose. Whether

you're aiming for physical health, career success, or emotional balance, your inner voice provides the roadmap. If
you ignore this guidance, you might find external reminders
appearing as life challenges, redirecting you toward your
true path.

When you set intentions and goals, choose your words
carefully. Instead of focusing on what you want to eliminate,
try framing your desires in terms of what you wish to gain
or become. For instance, rather than fixating on quitting
smoking, you might set your sights on achieving freedom
or embracing health. This subtle shift can align your mental
energy with positive outcomes.

Think of your mind as a navigation system, with your
desires setting the destination and your thoughts plotting
the course. Once you can clearly envision and articulate your
goals, your inner guidance system takes over. The key is to
trust this internal wisdom and follow its prompts, whether
it's urging you to take action, rest, or change direction.

However, remember the path to your goals isn't always
straightforward. You may encounter detours, face unexpected challenges, or temporarily lose your way. In these
moments, trust that your internal navigation system is
recalculating, offering new routes toward your destination. By clearly defining your destination, trusting your inner
guidance, and remaining open to the journey's twists and
turns, you align yourself with the natural flow of positive
change. This process is simple and universal, applicable to
any goal you might have.

Your mind, like a tireless navigator, continuously charts

your course through life. Even when you feel lost or off-track, your mind's navigational capacity remains intact, ready to redirect you toward your desired destination. Yet this powerful tool requires your active engagement. If you neglect its guidance or consistently ignore its prompts, this innate system can deteriorate. Don't let it!

Through it all, it's important to remind yourself that life isn't just about positive experiences. What you might quickly label as negative or undesirable could actually be a signpost guiding you toward your true desires. If you automatically reject these experiences, you might be dismissing the very catalysts you need for growth and fulfillment. This understanding explains why you might not see significant life changes, even when you're trying to maintain positive thoughts. Life is like a diverse gift package, filled with a range of experiences, emotions, and energies. Each element, regardless of how you initially perceive it, offers unique lessons and insights.

If you think of life as a journey and your desires as destinations, it's important to recognize that your aspirations are deeply personal and unique to you. They're not just goals, but energies that define and create who you are. The more intimately you understand and articulate your desires—their nuances, sensory details, and emotional resonance—the more effectively you can navigate toward them. This process is like providing a detailed address for a package delivery. Vague instructions might lead you astray, while a precise description ensures accurate arrival. Similarly, the clarity and specificity with which you define your goals significantly influence your ability to achieve them.

Listen, your desires aren't random. While themes like happiness, peace, love, and prosperity are universal, the specific ways you want these to manifest are unique to you. This individuality in your aspirations reflects the rich tapestry of your personal experience and potential. So, try to embrace both the positive and negative aspects of your journey equally. By clearly defining your unique desires, you open yourself to a more holistic approach to personal growth and goal achievement. This balanced perspective can help you navigate life's complexities with greater wisdom, recognizing that every experience, pleasant or challenging, contributes to your ultimate path of self-realization and fulfillment.

Your desires also reflect your unique essence. Your aspirations, whether for a specific car, a particular living environment, or personal attributes, are as varied as your physical characteristics. These differences stem from your distinct needs and the unique experiences you're meant to have in this world. That's because your desires are intrinsically linked to your purpose and personal journey. Just as you possess unique physical features, your wishes and goals are tailored to your individual path. You are essentially designed to pursue these personalized aspirations, with your life's trajectory naturally aligned to fulfill these desires.

All in all, the realization of your true wishes isn't miraculous—it's an inherent part of your life's design. Health, youthfulness, peace, and fulfillment are not unattainable ideals but natural states you're meant to experience. The challenge lies in recognizing and embracing your authentic path. As you continue on your journey of self-discovery and purpose, remember that every experience, whether perceived as positive or negative, contributes to your growth. Your purpose isn't a destination to reach, but a path to walk. It's about aligning your actions with your deepest values and desires and allowing your unique gifts to flourish.

Embrace the process of uncovering your purpose. Be patient with yourself as you explore, question, and evolve. Your purpose may shift and refine as you grow, and that's perfectly natural. The key is to remain open, attentive to your inner guidance, and willing to take action in alignment with your truest self.

By living with intention and embracing your unique journey, you not only fulfill your purpose but also contribute to the world in a way that only you can. Your purpose is your gift to yourself and the world—honor it, nurture it, and let it guide you to a life of meaning, fulfillment, and joy.

Sacred Reminders

+ Your purpose flows from your authentic self, not societal expectations. Trust that your unique way of contributing to the world is as natural as your fingerprint and just as distinctive.

+ As a woman, you've been deeply conditioned by society. Your journey to purpose requires consciously examining which beliefs are truly yours and which were imposed upon you. Let your intuition guide this unlearning.

+ Your purpose isn't fixed. In fact, it evolves as you grow. Like a river finding its course, your sense of meaning may shift and deepen over time. This evolution is not only natural but necessary for your expansion.

+ Your desires and aspirations are not random. They're instead signposts pointing you to your purpose. The unique way you wish to express universal themes like love, peace, and creativity reflects your soul's journey.

+ When aligned with your purpose, even challenges become meaningful stepping stones. Your inner compass will guide you through uncertainty, helping you navigate life's complexities with greater resilience and clarity.

Principle 5: Relationships

The purpose of this chapter is to educate you about relationships from the highest possible level of consciousness. We aim to help you understand how loving and balanced relationships can be experienced. This training will free you from the meanings you attribute to relationships and enable you to embark on a path to truly meet your soulmate.

So, how can we meet our soulmate, and why do we start relationship training with this idea? A soulmate is someone with whom we can establish a relationship that truly satisfies us at the highest level. If a person deepens their relationship with themselves and establishes a meaningful connection with their own soul, they will eventually reach a point where they can meet their soulmate.

But before we can meet our soulmate we must be able to allow another person to love us for who we are. This means we must first embrace both our strengths and weaknesses, and embark on a journey of self-awareness. It is crucial to understand this before discussing how to meet our soulmate. Achieving a high level of consciousness is essential to connect with anyone on a deeper level. That's because our connections transcend the physical realm and resonate through the depths of our souls. In this way, we share a profound bond that allows us to feel and know each other intimately as if we are reflections of one another.

When we consider the entirety of life, we should recognize that our experiences reflect our level of consciousness. It's important not to view relationships as a means to strengthen our connection with ourselves and our souls. Rather, it is the opposite: When we cultivate a strong connection with our essence and align ourselves with the truth, our soulmate will naturally appear in our lives.

When our soulmate comes into our lives, we are not on a quest to find happiness; rather, we seek to fulfill our own happiness so that our soulmate can join us in that joy. From my own experience, having gone through numerous relationships and two marriages, I can attest that to truly experience the highest level of satisfaction—at the heart and essence of our being—one must first find oneself.

Personally, I have been with my partner for twelve years. I feel a profound connection with him that transcends time—it's a deep bond of the heart, and he feels the same way. When I compare my relationship with my partner to other relationships I've had, it's clear that those others were merely friendships or superficial interactions. The connection with my soulmate is unlike anything I've experienced; it is deep, genuine, and truly intimate. But because we all seek this level of connection, if we are not experiencing it, we often feel a void or sense of dissatisfaction, even if it's slight.

Many of the feelings of emptiness or something being off in our current or past relationships arise from not having encountered our soulmate. The soulmate relationship is so uniquely satisfying that it allows for understanding beyond words. We share a bond that feels unbreakable, regardless of external circumstances. It's as if we exist in our own world.

Achieving this level of unity, harmony, and balance—without any gaps—is essential for finding real satisfaction in relationships. My goal is to help you reach this level because I have experienced it myself. Other teachers may offer various formulas for relationships, but it's crucial to understand that each relationship is unique, and the experience of a soulmate connection will vary from one person to another.

Rather than providing a set of formulas, I aim to guide you toward your inner self. That's because the connection with a soulmate shapes every aspect of life. When two people come together with their own identities, they create a powerful unity. In this relationship, being together allows for a profound experience of existence, reminiscent of how the universe consists of opposing forces—male and female, yin and yang. Genuine love emerges when these polarities coexist. True unity and spiritual fulfillment occur when we come together with that special someone. This concept is especially clear in intimate moments; the peak of sexual connection is when many experience a touch of the Divine.

Listen, being with a soulmate has the potential to transform your entire life. Those who find peace, happiness, and fulfillment within themselves, their marriage, and their home tend to be more successful in achieving their goals. We will explore the concept of soulmates further and through some exercises. When discussing soulmates, it's helpful to view women and men as representations of masculine and feminine energy. These energies are like two halves of an apple, reflecting the yin and yang balance present in the universe. Everything consists of these opposing forces, which always exist in equal amounts.

For instance, in quantum physics, the positive and negative poles of an atom are charged equally. This principle, supported by the laws proven by Einstein, shows that positive and negative energies are always in harmony. Similarly, masculine and feminine energies in the universe are always equal and complementary.

Human beings have depended on each other since the dawn of time, even partaking in the forbidden apple to complete one another. There is no singular existence in the universe; we are all searching for our other half. Unfortunately, many people are currently facing challenges in finding their soulmates. This often occurs because they haven't reached the level of consciousness needed to recognize their soulmates, or their connection to their own souls remains unfulfilled. As a result, they may feel stagnant or experience a decline in their lives.

Relationships are central to our existence, and we cannot resolve other life issues without first addressing them. Resolving relationship dynamics is the first step toward overcoming all other challenges in life. We must experience integration and connect with our truth, allowing masculine and feminine energies to complement one another.

✦

A soulmate reflects our connection with ourselves and our alignment with our true being. As I explained earlier, the more authentic we are, the more we live according to our values, and free from the patterns in our minds. This authenticity deepens our connection to our soul and essence, leading to relationships that mirror our true selves—be it with a partner, friends, or others.

✦

The process of aligning with ourselves is essential, and factors like our values and awakening play significant roles. Personally, my true life began in my thirties, aligning with the idea that true life starts around the age of thirty-five, as is believed by many spiritual leaders. The signs of this shift began fifteen years ago, but it fully materialized close to that age. However, if it hasn't happened for you yet, it may simply be delayed; that's perfectly normal. Don't worry!

So, what constitutes true life? It's a state where our alignment with our true selves is strong, providing clarity on who we are, our purpose in life, and what we are meant to do. In this state, we are free from the conditioning of the past. The more past patterns and limitations we carry, the less connected we are to ourselves.

As you progress through the awakening process and utilize methods like the Demartini Method, you will begin to experience what centering feels like. When we stay centered, our destiny, intentions, and desires come together as one. I've elaborated on this in my book *The Silence Revolution*, which I also recommend reading if you haven't yet.

Our destiny—what we are meant to live—is closely connected to our executive consciousness. When we operate from this state, we experience our true life—we meet our soulmates and become who we were meant to be, all in alignment with our soul groups and the life we were destined to live.

Recently, I mentored a friend, and like many others I've encountered, they described how their relationships usually begin on a very positive note. At the start, they often see one another as wonderful individuals. However, over time, either she grows distant, or they do. This illusion of love—focusing solely on the positive aspects of a person and expecting a one-sided experience—tends to be the root of the problem. No one is purely positive; if we perceive someone only as good, we must recognize that this is a distorted view. Otherwise, the relationship is likely to end sooner or later.

Love can become an illusion when we only acknowledge a person's admirable qualities and ignore their negative sides. If we don't maintain a neutral perspective, our view becomes easily skewed. This situation leads to extreme emotions and black-and-white thinking. Unfortunately, at the beginning of a relationship, we often view our partner as extraordinary and overlook potential downsides. For instance, if someone is strong, we might fail to see the negatives associated with that strength.

Why is this black-and-white thinking problematic? Because no behavior is one-sided. Every human trait has its drawbacks. When we choose certain qualities in a partner, we inevitably encounter trade-offs. For example, if you prefer a strong partner, you may find that they can be controlling or stubborn during disagreements. The negative side of strength is often a lack of flexibility in accepting differing opinions.

Conversely, when choosing a gentle and loving person, you might overlook their inability to assert themselves. This may lead to disappointment when you realize they are not as forceful or expressive in conflict situations. If we begin our relationships without a balanced perspective on the traits we desire, we may find ourselves surprised later on. However, if we acknowledge the potential downsides and are ready to confront them, we can navigate the relationship more successfully.

During love, it's easy to oscillate between extremes: seeing someone as entirely virtuous or completely flawed. When we view a person as solely good or perfectly beautiful, we disconnect from reality and enter a fantasy. Everyone possesses both commendable and less desirable traits. For instance, if you are drawn to a handsome or beautiful individual, it's crucial to acknowledge the potential negatives. They might be overly self-involved, spend excessive time preening themselves, or attract unwanted attention from others. These are often the costs of beauty and attractiveness. If you are prepared to accept these aspects and maintain a realistic perspective on what you want in a partner, then you are ready to pursue that relationship. Unfortunately, many individuals lack this grounded understanding when entering relationships, leading to confusion and disappointment.

I understand that some of you may still wonder why a specific relationship ended. There is one fundamental truth about relationships: If there is no real love, it will come to an end. I will say this again: If there is no real love, relationships end. Conversely, if there is true love—which comes from eternity and continues into eternity—a relationship will last forever. I reiterate this because many people hold onto the illusion that "I loved you very much, but it ended." In these cases, what you feel is not true love for that person. Instead, you may have admired them and attributed an exaggerated significance to their presence in your life. In other words, you may have only seen their positive traits and ignored their flaws. This distorted perception transforms a real person into a hero or an angel in your mind, which is why you cry and suffer in their absence.

We do not suffer when we are truly connected through love. So, if you find yourself crying over someone, it is likely that you do not have a real connection with them. The reason so many relationships break apart is that there is often no true love present. It is crucial to understand this thoroughly. Once you grasp this concept, you will begin to comprehend everything related to relationships.

So, why do so many relationships end? It often stems from distorted perspectives. We attribute too much meaning to others and fail to see them as they truly are, which prevents us from loving them genuinely. True love involves recognizing both the positive and negative aspects of a person and confronting their humanity as well as our own. When we do not judge, but rather acknowledge the full humanity of the person in front of us, we can truly feel for them. But this is not easy.

To transition to truth, we must start by getting to know ourselves. Throughout our childhood, we've been shaped by our parents and figures of authority regarding what is good or bad. To find our soulmate, it is essential to work on transforming these distorted beliefs.

With this, I encourage you to get a dedicated notebook for this relationship training. I have various exercises to help you work through and clarify the meanings you attribute to relationships. Let's begin!

Exercise 1

We all carry relationship experiences that stretch from the past into the present. Even those who haven't yet had such experiences hold dreams and thoughts about what they would like to live.

Take a notebook and set aside two pages. On the first page, write down everything you would like to experience in your relationships, capturing even the smallest details. You can list hundreds of things if you wish.

On the second page, write down everything you do not want to experience in a relationship. Again, be as detailed as possible and write down as many as you can.

Next, open a third page. From your list of things you want to experience, choose one and write it at the top of the page as a title. For example, you might write "Looking into each other's eyes with love" or "Sharing affectionate glances." Be sure to choose something you have experienced before.

Now, under this title, list at least 30 possible harms this experience could bring to you and your life, considering every area: money, work, career, social life, leadership, emotions, mental and physical health, personal growth, intelligence, family, relationships, and your relationship with yourself. Think not only about the harm in the moment it happened but also the ways it has affected you up until now.

Then, select one situation from your list of things you don't want to experience and write it as a heading. For instance, you might choose "arguing" or "shouting at each other." Recall times in your relationships when this occurred. Write down at least 30 benefits that came from this situation—again across all areas of life and in line with your values. Think of the benefits not only at the time but also the ones that have continued to this day.

Keep going with this exercise until the experiences you desire no longer hold a grip on you—until you can genuinely say, "It doesn't matter if this happens or not." At the same time, continue writing until you no longer resist the experiences you don't want, but instead find yourself open and even willing to live them.

Exercise 2

You may or may not be familiar with the Demartini Method. This is a unique approach to human perception developed by John Demartini. It offers techniques for managing one's outlook on individuals, circumstances, and occurrences that often manifest as challenges or areas of conflict in daily life. This methodology also provides tools to develop a more equilibrated viewpoint on any given life scenario, facilitating the resolution of emotional burdens, obstacles, or concerns within a brief timeframe. Notably, this approach has gained traction among various professionals, including those in healthcare, business leadership, and psychology. This is a foundational step in understanding the types of relationships we want. However, to truly balance our consciousness and reach the level necessary to meet our soulmate, deeper work is required.

The awakening process plays a crucial role in this journey. In this process, you learn about 44,000 human characteristics, actions, inactions, and behaviors, and how to work through them. Each of these characteristics exists within us. When we fail to recognize them—either due to arrogance or feelings of guilt and shame—we distort our consciousness, preventing us from living authentically and establishing spiritual connections. Achieving peace with each of these traits facilitates balance in our consciousness. Consequently, this work is extremely important. Ideally, we should examine each of these 44,000 behaviors individually. However, many people tend to label a significant portion of them as either good or bad, which leads to a misunderstanding of our areas for growth.

Set aside two pages in your notebook. On the first page, write down the negative behaviors you have encountered in relationships: traits you believe exist in others but not in yourself. For example, you might write: "Ahmet was very rude, but I am not that rude," or "Ali was a liar, but I am not a liar," or "Ayşe was easily deceived, but I am not like that." Go as far back in your memories as you can to build this list.

Once you have your list, choose one trait. For instance: "Ahmet is rude, I am not; I am polite, he is rude." Then, go back through your life and find at least twenty different times when you demonstrated the same or a similar behavior: moments when you, too, were rude. In other words, identify twenty separate instances when you expressed that very trait. Keep doing this exercise until you can clearly see and fully understand that the same qualities you criticize, notice in your partner, or believe you do not have, actually exist within you in equal measure and number. For example: "When I was 15, I was rude to my mother; when I was 5, I was rude to my sister; when I was 10, I was rude to my classmate." Be sure to write down all these memories.

On the second page, write down the positive qualities you see in others that you believe you lack. Think of people you admire and note the traits you value in them but don't recognize in yourself. Then, choose one quality and recall twenty different times in your past when you actually displayed that very behavior. For example, you might think: "Ahmet is very polite, but I'm not." Look back and identify at least twenty moments when you were polite, and write them down. Continue this practice until you realize that you are just as polite as Ahmet.

Next, conduct a benefit-loss analysis based on these traits. This exercise will help you identify how much distortion exists in your mind and how long it has persisted. We must recognize that we have a long way to go to reach the level of consciousness we desire, and there is still much work ahead.

✦

Experiencing genuine love and affection is one of the highest challenges in this world. We carry so many distorted thoughts, conditionings, and memories from our past—be it from parents, childhood, or friendships—that love can easily get lost among them. Instead of claiming we cannot see the real person before us, we should focus on loving them. This journey is a process that requires understanding and commitment.

Trainings like relationship coaching, which start with strategic planning, help to highlight and clarify these issues. Why are these trainings important? They help us understand what steps we need to take to resolve our problems. Action plans enable us to identify where we need to invest our time and effort and address our personal deficiencies to better navigate our relationships.

Again, if you view someone through a distorted lens—whether judging them harshly or idolizing them without regard for their flaws—you are not experiencing real love. True love exists when we recognize the humanity in others and acknowledge all of their qualities and our shared characteristics. This understanding cultivates equality and balance in our relationships. As friendships, partnerships, and even marriages progress, they thrive on this foundation of shared humanity. If we disconnect from our essence and our sense of balance, we struggle to create meaningful relationships across the board. In my exploration of loneliness, I have observed that many people suffer from this disconnect, which inhibits their ability to form genuine connections. But remember, the first real connection must be with yourself.

Sacred Reminders

✦ To meet your soulmate, you must first develop a deep connection with yourself and your own soul. Self-awareness and self-acceptance are crucial steps in this process.

✦ True soulmate relationships are characterized by a profound, intimate bond that transcends ordinary connections. They offer a unique level of fulfillment and understanding.

✦ Balancing masculine and feminine energies is essential for achieving unity and hallowed health in relationships. These energies complement each other, reflecting the yin and yang balance in the universe.

✦ Resolving relationship dynamics is fundamental to overcoming other life challenges. Our relationships are central to our existence and personal growth.

✦ To elevate your consciousness and prepare for a soulmate relationship, it's important to examine and balance your perceptions of 44,000 human characteristics, actions, and behaviors.

✦ True love involves recognizing both the positive and negative aspects of a person. Seeing someone only in a positive light or focusing solely on their flaws leads to distorted perceptions and unsustainable relationships.

✦ If a relationship ends, it's often because true love is not present. Real love, which comes from eternity, sustains relationships indefinitely.

✦ Authentic relationships thrive on acknowledging our shared humanity and cultivating equality and balance. This understanding helps us form genuine connections and overcome feelings of loneliness.

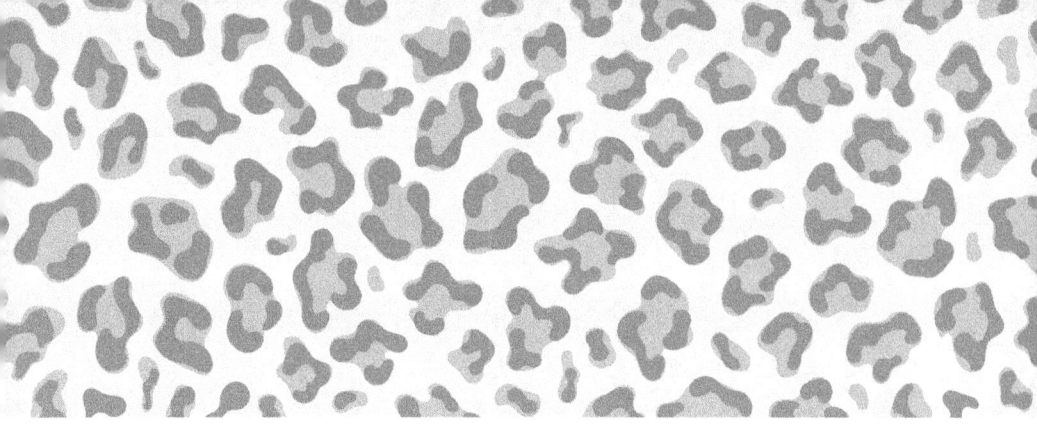

PART 3:

Living as a Goddess

The Art of Silence:
Your Gateway to Power

It was a crisp autumn morning in London when I witnessed something that would forever change my understanding of feminine power. I was sitting in a boardroom, watching two women navigate a complex negotiation. The first woman, whom I'll call Sarah, was doing everything she'd been taught about wielding power in the corporate world—speaking assertively, presenting logical arguments, filling every moment with words and action. The other woman, Elena, barely spoke at all. She sat in complete stillness, fully present but utterly quiet. When she did speak, her words emerged from a deep well of silence. They carried a weight that Sarah's rapid-fire communication could never achieve.

By the end of that meeting, Elena had accomplished everything she'd come for, while Sarah left frustrated and depleted. It wasn't Elena's words that had created this outcome—it was her silence. This scene plays out in different ways every day, in boardrooms and living rooms, in relationships and careers. Women have been taught that power comes through expression, through making ourselves heard, and through pushing our ideas forward. We've been conditioned to believe that silence means weakness, submission, or lack of authority. But what if we've fundamentally misunderstood the nature of silence?

In my work with thousands of women across the globe, I've observed a striking pattern: The most powerful women I encounter are not those who speak the most, but those who have mastered the art of silence. Not the empty silence of suppression, but the rich, fertile silence from which all creation emerges.

Think about the most powerful forces in nature. The gravitational pull of the moon doesn't announce itself with noise, yet it moves entire oceans. The roots of a tree grow in perfect silence, yet they can break through concrete. The transformation of a caterpillar into a butterfly happens in the quiet darkness of the cocoon. This is the kind of silence I'm inviting you to discover—not an absence, but a presence. Not a void, but a fullness. Not a restriction, but an expansion into your true power.

As one of my students once remarked after experiencing this deeper silence: "For the first time in my life, I understand why every great spiritual tradition speaks of silence as golden. It's not just golden—it's absolutely magical." But before we explore how to access and use this power, we must first understand what stands in our way.

In today's world, constant noise isn't just external—it has become our internal state of being. We've lost touch with silence because we've lost trust in our own depths. We fill every moment with words, with activity, with noise, because we're afraid of what we might find in the quiet.

But this fear isn't an accident or coincidence. A woman who has rediscovered the power of her silence is unstoppable. She becomes magnetic, naturally drawing to herself everything she needs. She develops an authority that doesn't need to announce itself. She accesses wisdom that goes far beyond what can be learned through external sources. In this section, I'll share with you the practical pathway to reclaiming this power. You'll learn why silence is particularly crucial for women, how to distinguish between empowering and disempowering silence, and specific practices for cultivating the kind of silence that amplifies your natural feminine power. But first, let's explore what happens when a woman begins to remember this forgotten art.

The Difference Between Empty Silence and Fertile Silence

When a woman becomes disconnected from her true power, the first sign is almost always in her speech. She begins to talk more, explain more, justify more. The more she talks, the more she loses her connection to the sacred feminine energy that is her birthright. I see this pattern repeated endlessly in my work, women who have been conditioned to believe that power comes through words, through constant expression, through endless explanation.

But look at Mother Nature. She teaches us a different truth. Nature doesn't explain herself. She doesn't justify her cycles or defend her rhythms. She simply is. And in that pure being-ness, she expresses a power that no amount of words could ever convey. This is our natural state as women. When we're aligned with our feminine essence, we don't need many words. Our presence speaks for itself. Our energy communicates without sound. Our wisdom flows not through endless discussion but through deep knowing.

I witnessed this transformation in one of my students who came to me as a successful corporate lawyer. She prided herself on her ability to outtalk anyone in the room. She won arguments through sheer verbal force. But she was exhausted, disconnected, and despite her outer success, deeply unfulfilled. Through our work together, she began to discover the power of silence. At first, it terrified her. Like many women, she had been using words as a shield, as a way to prove her worth, as a defense against vulnerability. But as she learned to trust the silence, something remark-able happened. Her presence in meetings became more powerful, not less. Her relationships deepened. Her creative energy flourished.

This is because true feminine power doesn't need to announce itself. When a woman is connected to her essence, aligned with her truth, she naturally emanates an energy that affects everything around her. She doesn't need to fill the space with words because she has learned to trust that her presence alone is enough.

But understand this: I'm not speaking about the silence of suppression that has been forced upon women throughout history. That silence comes from fear and disempowerment.

The silence I'm speaking of comes from a place of deep connection to your wisdom, your truth, and your power. It's the silence of the priestess, the queen, the woman who knows who she is and therefore has no need to constantly prove herself through words.

How Silence Connects Us to Our Feminine Essence

The relationship between silence and feminine essence is profound yet simple: Silence is the doorway through which we return to our true nature. When a woman stops talking, stops doing, stops trying to prove herself to the world, something extraordinary happens—she begins to remember who she really is. In the depths of silence, we discover that we are not what we've been trying so hard to be. We are not our achievements or our struggles. We are not our endless doing and striving. We are something far more profound—we are the creative force itself, the womb of all possibility.

This is why in ancient feminine mystery schools, the first teaching was always silence. Before a woman could access her true power, she had to learn to be still, to turn inward, to disconnect from the noise of the world. This wasn't about silencing women—it was about helping them discover their innate power.

When we are constantly speaking, constantly in motion, constantly engaging with the outer world, we can't hear the deeper wisdom that speaks through us. It's like trying to see your reflection in water that's constantly being stirred—the image is always distorted. But when the water becomes still, the reflection becomes clear. This stillness, this silence, is our natural state as women. We are designed to operate from a place of deep inner quiet, where intuition flows freely and wisdom arises naturally. This is why women who maintain a regular meditation practice often report feeling more like themselves. They are simply returning to their natural state of being.

But this connection goes even deeper. Our wombs, the sacred space within us that mirrors the creative force of the universe, operate in perfect silence. New life forms grow in silence. Transformation happens in silence. Creation itself emerges from silence. When we return to silence, we align ourselves with this creative power. But the modern world has taught us to fear silence and to fill every moment with noise and activity. But for a woman, this constant noise creates a profound disconnection from her essence. It's like trying to hear a subtle melody while standing next to a blaring loudspeaker—the deeper music of our being gets drowned out by the clamor of surface activity.

This is why the journey back to feminine essence must begin with silence. Not as a discipline to be mastered, but as a natural state to be remembered. Not as something we do, but as something we allow ourselves to return to. When we embrace silence, we create the space for our true nature to emerge. In silence, we discover that we don't need to prove our worth—it is inherent in our being. We don't need to fight for our power—it flows naturally when we stop blocking it with constant noise. We don't need to explain ourselves—our presence speaks more eloquently than words ever could. This is the gift of silence—it returns us to ourselves.

The Relationship Between Silence and Feminine Magnetism

The relationship between silence and feminine magnetism is one of the most misunderstood aspects of feminine power. Modern society has taught women that to attract what they want—whether in relationships, careers, or any other area of life—they need to speak up, put themselves forward, and make their desires known. In other words, be verbally assertive at all costs. Yet paradoxically, this very effort often pushes away the very things we're trying to attract.

Think of how nature works. A flower doesn't call out to the bees. Its very presence, its essence, naturally draws what it needs. The moon doesn't shout to move the tides. Its silent magnetic force effortlessly creates movement across every ocean on Earth. This is true feminine magnetism—the power to attract through presence rather than pursuit. When a woman discovers this truth, everything changes. I've seen this transformation countless times in my work. Women who have been exhausting themselves trying to make things happen suddenly discover that when they become silent and centered, life begins to flow to them naturally.

Consider what happens in relationships. When a woman is constantly talking, explaining, and trying to make her partner understand her needs. What she's actually operating in is masculine energy. She becomes the pursuer, the doer, the one making effort. But when she learns to rest in silence, to trust her magnetic presence, something shifts. Her partner naturally begins to move toward her, drawn by the mysterious power of her feminine essence.

This same principle applies in every area of life. In business, the woman who has mastered silence often finds she doesn't need to push for opportunities—they come to her. In creativity, ideas flow naturally when we stop forcing them and instead create space through silence. Even in healing, the deepest transformations often happen not through endless processing and talking, but through moments of profound silence.

But this magnetic silence isn't passive. And it's not about becoming a doormat or suppressing your truth. Instead, it's about accessing a deeper power—the power of being rather than doing, of attracting rather than pursuing, of allowing rather than forcing.

The key to developing this magnetic quality lies in understanding that true silence isn't empty—it's full. When a woman is silent but connected to her essence, she creates a field around her that others can feel. This is why in ancient traditions, the most powerful priestesses were often the most silent. Their very presence was magnetic because they weren't dissipating their energy through constant speech and activity.

Yet in today's world, many women fear this silence. They worry that if they stop talking, stop pushing, stop doing, they'll become invisible. The opposite is true. When a woman learns to rest in profound silence, she becomes more visible than ever—not to the physical eye perhaps, but to the deeper sense that recognizes true power.

This magnetic quality cannot be faked. It comes only through a genuine connection to your feminine essence, which is found in the depths of silence. When you're truly aligned with this power, you don't need to announce yourself or push yourself forward. Like the moon moving the tides, your very presence creates movement in the world around you.

How to Cultivate Powerful Silence

Cultivating powerful feminine silence isn't about imposing rigid disciplines on yourself or forcing yourself to be quiet. Rather, it's about creating the conditions that allow natural silence to emerge. Let me share with you the practical pathway that has transformed countless women's relationships with silence.

The first step is understanding when to be silent. This isn't about never speaking. On the contrary, it's about recognizing those moments when speech diminishes your power rather than enhances it. When you feel the urge to explain yourself repeatedly, to fill empty space with words, to speak from anxiety rather than clarity—these are the moments calling for silence. Begin by observing yourself in daily life. Notice when you speak from your center and when you speak from your edges. Notice how your energy feels after long periods of talking versus periods of chosen silence. Pay attention to how others respond to your words versus your silent presence.

The practice of meditation is essential here, but not in the way most people approach it. For women, meditation isn't about forcing the mind into silence—it's about allowing ourselves to sink back into our natural state of being. Start with just twenty minutes each morning and evening. Close your eyes and simply be with yourself. Don't try to stop your thoughts or create any particular state. Just rest in your own presence.

In your daily interactions, practice what I call the *pause of power*. Before responding to any situation, take a conscious breath and allow yourself to feel into your center. This brief moment of silence can shift the entire dynamic of a conversation or decision. You'll find that when your words emerge from silence rather than reaction, they carry far more weight.

Create regular periods of sacred silence in your life. This might mean turning off your phone for certain hours, spending time in nature without speaking, or simply sitting quietly with a cup of tea before starting your day. These aren't restrictions. They're gifts you give yourself, opportunities to reconnect with your essence.

Practice listening not just to others, but to the silence itself. In this deep listening, you'll begin to hear the wisdom that has always been waiting for you in the quiet. This is where your intuition speaks most clearly, where your true knowing emerges.

Pay particular attention to your relationship with silence in challenging situations. When someone criticizes you, when you feel unseen or unheard, when you're facing important decisions—these are the moments when maintaining your connection to silence is most crucial and most powerful.

Again, remember that silence doesn't mean becoming passive. In fact, it's quite the opposite. When you're truly resting in powerful silence, you're deeply engaged with life, but from a place of centered presence rather than anxious doing. Your actions emerge naturally from this silence, carrying the full weight of your feminine power.

Most importantly, be patient with yourself in this practice. The world pulls us constantly toward noise and activity. Returning to silence is like building a muscle, it strengthens over time with consistent, gentle practice. Each time you choose silence over unnecessary speech, you're strengthening your connection to your feminine essence.

✦

The ultimate practice is learning to carry silence within you even while engaging with the world. This is the mark of a woman fully in her power because she can speak, act, and engage while maintaining her connection to the deep well of silence at her core. From this place, everything becomes possible. Your presence becomes magnetic, your words carry weight, and your very being becomes a force for transformation in the world.

This is your birthright as a woman. This is the power that awaits you in silence.

Sacred Reminders

✦ Remember that your silence carries more power
than a thousand words spoken without presence.
Like the moon moving oceans without a sound,
your centered silence naturally moves the world
around you.

✦ Remember that when you rest in true silence, you
are not empty but full, as full as the sacred womb
space from which all creation emerges. This is
not the silence of suppression but the silence of
infinite potential.

✦ Remember that your essence communicates
without words. When you're aligned with your
feminine nature, your very presence speaks
volumes. Trust this. There is no need to explain,
defend, or justify.

✦ Remember that power flows naturally when
you dare to be still. The more deeply you trust
silence, the more effortlessly life responds to your
unspoken intentions.

✦ Remember that this practice isn't about silencing
your voice. It's about ensuring that when you do
speak, your words carry the full weight of your
feminine wisdom and power.

Beyond the Five Senses

The morning sun streams through my window in Istanbul, warming my face. But I don't merely feel its physical touch. I sense its presence at a level far deeper than skin. This is how a woman naturally experiences the world when she remembers her true nature: not through the limited portal of physical sensation, but through the vast expanse of feminine knowing.

As women, we have been taught to rely primarily on our five senses, to trust only what we can see, hear, touch, taste, and smell. Yet this represents a profound misunderstanding of feminine power. A woman's natural state of being exists beyond the physical realm, in a dimension where intuitive wisdom flows freely and where we can access depths of knowing that transcend ordinary perception.

This section explores how women can reclaim their innate ability to operate beyond the five senses and why doing so is essential for accessing our full creative power. We'll examine why getting caught in purely physical perception diminishes feminine energy, and how transcending the sensory world allows us to step into our role as channels for sacred wisdom and creation.

The journey beyond the five senses represents one of the most crucial shifts a woman can make from living as a purely physical being to embodying her nature as a spiritual force. When we learn to disengage from constant sensory input and access deeper ways of knowing, we open ourselves to levels of power, wisdom, and creative capacity that are our natural birthright. This goes far beyond simply developing intuition or psychic abilities. It's about fundamentally shifting how we engage with reality—from operating primarily through physical perception to allowing our consciousness to expand into realms where the feminine naturally thrives. When we make this shift, we discover that what we thought were our limitations were merely the boundaries of the physical world, not the true scope of our feminine potential.

The practices and principles in this section will guide you in making this essential transition. You'll learn how to recognize when you're caught in purely physical perception, how to access expanded states of feminine knowing, and how to navigate life increasingly from this broader perspective. This represents a radical departure from how most modern women have been taught to function, but it is the key to reclaiming our most natural and powerful way of being.

Let us begin this exploration of the vast territory that lies beyond our physical senses—the domain where feminine power truly comes alive.

How Women Naturally Operate Beyond the Physical Realm

Picture a master weaver working at her loom. While her hands move through the physical motions of weaving, her awareness extends far beyond her fingers. She perceives the emerging pattern not just with her eyes, but with an inner vision that sees the full tapestry before it materializes. This is how women naturally operate—simultaneously present in the physical world while accessing deeper realms of knowing and creation.

The truth is we were never meant to be confined to purely physical perception. Just as our wombs can create new life, a process that transcends ordinary physical laws, our consciousness naturally extends beyond the material plane. This is not mystical thinking, but rather our most natural state of being. Consider how often you've known something without knowing how you knew it. Perhaps you sensed when your child was in distress even though you were miles away. Or you knew exactly when to call a friend who needed you, without any external prompt. These aren't coincidences or lucky guesses. They're glimpses of how women naturally perceive and operate when we're not locked into purely physical sensing.

But in today's world, we've been trained to doubt these deeper ways of knowing. We've learned to trust only what we can measure, see, or prove through physical means. This has cut us off from vast reservoirs of feminine wisdom and power. It's like trying to navigate using only a flashlight when we naturally possess night vision. In doing so, we forget that we can see in the dark. And the consequences of this forgetting are profound. When we rely solely on physical perception, we become exhausted trying to figure everything out through mental processing alone. Our natural creative abilities become blocked as we ignore the subtle channels through which inspiration naturally flows. We lose touch with our innate wisdom, leading our bodies to manifest illness and imbalance. Our relationships suffer because we can't access the deeper levels of understanding that allow for true connection. This is why so many women feel constantly drained and disconnected. We're operating in a way that goes against our natural design. We're like fish who've forgotten we can swim, struggling to walk on land.

The good news is that this capacity to operate beyond physical sensing never actually leaves us, it simply goes dormant. And like any natural ability, it can be reawakened through conscious practice and awareness. Take Maria, one of my students who came to me utterly exhausted from trying to manage her international business through pure mental effort and physical action. She'd been taught this was the only professional way to operate. But as she learned to access her natural feminine perception, everything shifted. She began knowing which opportunities to pursue without endless analysis. She could sense when deals would work out and when they wouldn't. Her business flourished even as she worked less because she was operating from her natural feminine capacity rather than trying to function like a man.

This is available to all of us. When we remember how to operate beyond physical sensing, we discover an entirely new way of being in the world. Solutions arise naturally without mental strain, and we develop an innate knowing of exactly when to act and when to wait. Our creativity flows effortlessly as we access deeper wells of inspiration. Our relationships deepen and become more authentic as we perceive beyond surface interactions. Our health improves as we align with our natural way of being. And we access levels of wisdom and knowing that transcend ordinary perception.

This isn't about denying or escaping the physical world. It's about expanding beyond its limitations while remaining fully present in our bodies. It's about reclaiming our natural capacity to perceive and operate on multiple levels simultaneously.

The Two Realities: The Masculine Physical and The Feminine Spiritual

To understand how women naturally operate beyond the five senses, we must first understand a fundamental truth: Men and women experience reality in profoundly different ways. This isn't about gender stereotypes or social conditioning. Rather, it's about the essential nature of masculine and feminine energy.

Imagine two people observing a garden. The masculine eye sees the physical structure—the arrangement of plants, the geometry of paths, and the mechanics of the irrigation system. The feminine consciousness experiences something far broader—the flow of life force through the plants, the subtle interplay of energies, and the garden's connection to the wider web of life. Neither perspective is wrong; they are complementary ways of perceiving the same reality.

The masculine naturally excels in the physical realm. This is why men build extraordinary systems and structures, creating the frameworks that organize our material world. They thrive on concrete action, measurable results, and tangible achievements. Their natural gifts serve an essential purpose in the physical dimension.

But we women have been pressured to adopt this masculine way of perceiving and operating in the world, and it's taking a tremendous toll. When we try to function primarily through physical sensing and logical analysis, we cut ourselves off from our natural power source. It's like trying to run a solar panel in the shade, we're simply not designed to operate this way.

I see this regularly in my practice. Women come to me exhausted from trying to succeed using masculine methods—pushing, striving, and relying solely on physical action and mental analysis. They've been taught this is what it means to be professional or effective. But the more they push in this direction, the more depleted they become.

What they don't realize is that feminine power operates through a completely different channel. While masculine energy excels in the physical dimension, feminine energy naturally flows in the spiritual dimension—the realm beyond physical sensing where creation itself originates. This is why women throughout history have been the mystics, the seers, the keepers of wisdom that transcends ordinary knowing.

Think of how a pregnant woman knows things about her unborn child that no medical test can detect. Or how a mother instantly knows when her child is in danger, even from miles away. These aren't anomalies or supernatural powers. They're glimpses of how women naturally perceive when we're operating from our feminine essence. This feminine way of knowing isn't vague or impractical. In fact, it's extraordinarily precise and effective, but in a different way than masculine knowing. While masculine perception excels at analyzing what already exists in the physical world, feminine perception can sense what's emerging, what wants to be created, and what lies just beyond the threshold of manifestation.

I witnessed this profound difference through my own journey. For years, I tried to succeed in business using purely masculine methods—detailed analysis, aggressive action, and relying solely on what I could see and measure. I achieved results but at a tremendous cost to my energy and well-being. Everything changed when I remembered my natural feminine way of operating. Now I navigate business decisions through a combination of practical analysis and deeper feminine knowing. I can sense which opportunities align with creation's flow and which don't, often before any physical evidence exists. This isn't about replacing practical action but about accessing a broader field of information and operating from a more expansive reality.

The Trap of Sensory Perception

I remember the moment I first understood how deeply we've been caught in the trap of physical sensing. I was sitting in my garden in Istanbul, obsessing over every detail of an upcoming project. I was analyzing, planning, and trying to control every variable through mental effort. Then suddenly, I became aware of how contracted my energy had become, how I'd shrunk myself down to fit within the narrow confines of physical perception. This is what happens when we become entrapped by the five senses—we reduce ourselves to a fraction of our true capacity. It's like trying to understand the ocean by examining only the waves on the surface, completely forgetting the vast depths below.

The signs of this sensory entrapment are everywhere in women's lives today. We see it in the constant anxiety about physical appearance, the exhausting effort to control everything through action, and the endless chatter that fills every silence. These are all symptoms of having lost connection with our deeper way of knowing and being. When we're caught in pure sensory perception, we become like leaves blown about by every wind—reactive, unstable, and easily thrown off center. Every sight, sound, taste, touch, and smell demands our attention and response. We lose our natural ability to remain rooted in deeper truth while engaging with the physical world.

I see this particularly clearly in my work with women in leadership positions. Many come to me wondering why they feel so drained despite their success. Invariably, I discover they're operating almost entirely through physical sensing and mental processing. They've learned to ignore their deeper knowing in favor of what can be proven through external evidence. The cost of this sensory imprisonment is profound. Our bodies begin to manifest illness because we've cut ourselves off from the natural flow of healing energy. Our relationships become superficial because we're engaging only at the physical level rather than through deeper feminine knowing. And our creative power diminishes because we've lost access to the subtle realms where true creation originates.

Consider Sarah, a brilliant executive who came to me struggling with chronic fatigue and recurring health issues despite having the so-called perfect diet and exercise routine. Through our work together, she realized she'd become so focused on managing physical reality that she'd completely lost touch with her body's deeper wisdom. She was literally unable to sense what her body truly needed because she'd become locked in physical perception. As she learned to operate beyond the five senses, everything changed. Not only did her health improve, but she discovered she could accomplish more with less effort. Instead of pushing through physical action alone, she learned to sense the natural flow of energy and align her actions accordingly. Ultimately, her leadership transformed as she accessed deeper levels of knowledge about her team and organization.

This is what becomes possible when we free ourselves from the prison of pure sensory perception. We discover that what we thought were limitations were just the boundaries of physical reality. Beyond these boundaries lies our natural domain as women—the vast realm of spiritual perception where true power resides.

Practices for Accessing Deeper Feminine Knowing

The journey beyond the five senses isn't a distant spiritual ideal. It's a practical path that begins with simple yet profound practices. I discovered this truth through years of working with women from all walks of life. The methods I'll share aren't complicated, but they require something more challenging than complex techniques. They require trust in your deeper knowing.

Let's begin with the most essential practice: conscious disconnection from sensory input. This doesn't mean withdrawing from life, but rather creating deliberate periods of time when you step back from the constant flood of physical stimulation. For example, start your day with twenty minutes of sitting in silence, eyes closed, before engaging with the world. This isn't about forcing your mind to be quiet. It's about allowing yourself to settle into the deeper current of feminine knowing that lies beneath surface perception.

I learned the power of this practice during a transformative period in my own life. After years of pushing myself to exhaustion, I began dedicating the first moments of each day to sitting in silence. At first, it felt like wasted time. But gradually, I discovered that these moments of conscious disconnection from sensory input enhanced my ability to navigate the physical world with grace and wisdom.

The second essential practice is what I call centering in the womb space. Place your attention in the area of your lower belly, the sacred center of feminine creating. This isn't just a physical focus. It's about shifting your consciousness from head to center, from thinking to knowing. Throughout your day, especially when feeling overwhelmed by sensory input or facing important decisions, bring your attention back to this center.

Ilya, a surgeon I worked with, initially resisted this practice. "I need to stay in my head to do my work," she insisted. But as she learned to operate from her center while maintaining her technical expertise, she found her surgical intuition becoming remarkably enhanced. She knew exactly what her patients needed beyond what the tests showed. Her practice transformed as she accessed this deeper way of knowing.

The third practice involves consciously shifting from external to internal guidance. When facing a decision or challenge, instead of gathering more external information or asking others' opinions, pause and ask yourself: What do I know about this from my deeper wisdom? Then wait, staying centered in your body, allowing the knowing to emerge naturally. This might feel uncomfortable at first as we've been trained to distrust our inner knowing. But with practice, you'll discover this guidance is remarkably reliable.

Remember, these practices aren't about replacing practical action or analytical thinking. They're about accessing additional layers of information and operating from a more complete way of knowing. You'll still use your five senses, but they'll no longer be your only source of information about reality.

As you develop these practices, you'll likely encounter resistance—both from within yourself and from others. The world isn't always comfortable with women who operate beyond ordinary perception. Trust this process anyway. You're not learning something new. You're remembering your natural way of being.

But start small. Begin with five minutes of silence each morning. Practice returning to your center three times each day. Listen to your deeper knowledge about small decisions before moving to larger ones. Notice how your body feels when you're operating from physical sensing alone versus when you're accessing deeper knowing.

Most importantly, remember that this journey beyond the five senses isn't about reaching some distant destination. It's about returning to your natural way of being as a woman. The more you practice, the more you'll recognize that you've always known how to operate this way. That you're simply remembering what you've temporarily forgotten.

Above all, trust this journey. Trust your knowing. Trust the wisdom that flows through you when you allow yourself to operate beyond ordinary perception. This is your birthright as a woman this ability to access and operate from levels of reality that transcend the physical world.

Sacred Reminders

✦ Trust your internal knowledge over external evidence. What you sense beyond the physical is your greatest truth.

✦ Your womb carries wisdom deeper than any thought. Return to this center and let it guide you.

✦ When you find yourself striving through physical effort, pause. True feminine power flows from stillness.

✦ The world has nothing to give you that surpasses what you already hold within. Remember this when external reality tries to seduce your attention.

✦ Release the need to prove what you know through your five senses. The deepest feminine wisdom cannot be measured, only known.

The Flow of Creation

I stand at my window watching leaves dance in the breeze. They don't strive or strain. They simply allow themselves to be moved by currents of air too subtle for the eye to see. This is how creation naturally works through the feminine—not through force or effort, but through alignment with invisible flows of energy that shape our reality.

As women, we've been taught that creation requires pushing, planning, and striving—the masculine way of bringing things into being. We've learned to set goals, make detailed plans, and force our way forward through sheer determination. But this approach betrays our natural feminine way of creating, which flows as effortlessly as water finding its path to the sea.

This isn't about eschewing action or abandoning our aims. Rather, it's about understanding that feminine creation operates through different laws than masculine manifestation. While masculine energy excels at building through focused effort and systematic action, feminine energy creates through surrender, through allowing, through becoming a channel for what wants to emerge through us.

For instance, think of how a woman's body creates new life. Though we can support the process, we don't actually do the creating—we allow it to happen through us. Our wombs know exactly how to weave a new being into existence without our conscious direction. This same wisdom, this same capacity to allow creation to flow through us, exists in every area of our lives. But only if we remember how to access it.

In this section, we'll explore the profound difference between masculine manifestation and feminine creation. You'll discover why trying to create through pure effort leaves you exhausted and disconnected from your natural power. Most importantly, you'll learn how to shift from pushing things into being to allowing them to flow through you—the natural feminine way of creating that you've always known but may have forgotten.

Let us begin this journey into the deep waters of feminine creation, where effort gives way to flow, and pushing is replaced by profound allowing.

The Dance of Creation:
Masculine and Feminine Ways

The masculine creates in straight lines. The feminine creates in spirals. This fundamental difference shapes everything about how men and women naturally bring things into being.

Consider how a man typically approaches creation. He sets a clear target, plots the most direct path, and moves systematically toward his goal. Like an archer aiming at a distant mark, he focuses his energy on a precise line of action. This approach serves him well because it aligns with masculine energy's natural gifts for focused action and systematic progress.

But when women try to create this way, something essential is lost. I see this repeatedly in my work with female entrepreneurs and leaders. They come to me exhausted from trying to force their creations into being through pure willpower and strategic action. They've learned to set SMART goals, create detailed action plans, and push relentlessly forward. Yet despite their efforts, their creations feel hollow, lacking the aliveness that comes when we create in alignment with our feminine nature.

That's because the feminine creates differently. Rather than aiming at a fixed target, we attune ourselves to what wants to emerge through us. Instead of forcing a straight path forward, we spiral inward to connect with deeper currents of creative energy and then allow these currents to move through us. This isn't passive as it requires profound presence and trust. But it's fundamentally different from masculine-focused action.

I witnessed this contrast vividly during a recent business meeting. My male partners were focused on strategic planning and mapping out every step of our next project. While I honored their approach, I stayed connected to a deeper knowing of what wanted to emerge. When I sensed the moment was right, I shared a vision that had come to me about the project's direction. The vision didn't emerge from analysis, it arose from staying attuned to creative flow. My partners immediately recognized its wisdom, even though it couldn't have been reached through strategic planning alone.

This is how feminine creation works—not through forcing and pushing, but through attunement and allowing. When a woman creates in alignment with her nature, she becomes like a musical instrument through which the universe plays its song. The creation flows through her rather than from her. This doesn't mean she takes no action. But rather her actions arise from alignment rather than force.

Think of how water creates. It doesn't push against obstacles, it flows around them, finding the path of least resistance. Yet over time, water shapes mountains. This is feminine creative power, achieved not through force but through persistent, graceful flow.

✦

The masculine builds structures; the feminine creates life. The masculine manifests through focused will; the feminine creates through surrender to what wants to be born. Both approaches are valid and necessary, but as women, we must remember our natural way of creating. When we try to create like men, we exhaust ourselves and diminish the power of what wants to emerge through us.

Cocreating with Universal Forces

Imagine sitting by a river. You can wade in and try to push the water where you want it to go, exhausting yourself while accomplishing little. Or you can study the river's natural flows and patterns, and then place your paddle in just the right spot to harness its power. This is the difference between trying to force creation and learning to cocreate with universal forces.

As women, we are natural cocreators. Our bodies know how to work with the forces of creation to bring new life into being. This same capacity extends to everything we create, but we must remember how to access it. The key lies in understanding that true creative power doesn't originate from our individual will or effort. Rather, it flows through us when we align ourselves with larger creative forces. This isn't mystical thinking. It's practical wisdom about how feminine creation actually works.

I learned this lesson deeply during my early years in business. I would push and strain to make things happen, work endless hours, and try to control every detail. The results were mediocre at best. Everything changed when I remembered my natural feminine way of creating. Instead of forcing things into being, I began listening deeply to what wanted to emerge. I discovered that when I stayed aligned with my center and trusted my inner knowing, opportunities would arise naturally. The right people would appear at precisely the right moment. Solutions would emerge effortlessly that no amount of strategic planning could have devised.

This isn't about becoming passive. Cocreating requires profound presence and discernment. We must learn to distinguish between the authentic, creative current and the numerous distractions that can pull us off course. We must develop the courage to follow what we sense even when it defies conventional logic.

Consider how a pregnant woman knows exactly what her body needs, moment by moment, to support the new life growing within her. She doesn't arrive at this knowledge through research or analysis. No, it arises naturally when she stays connected to her inner wisdom. This same knowing is available to us in everything we create, whether it's a business, a work of art, or a new way of living.

The practice of cocreating begins with stillness. We must first quiet the noise of our striving mind to sense the deeper currents of creative energy. This is why meditation isn't just a spiritual practice. It's rather a practical training in becoming a clear channel for creation to flow through. From this place of inner stillness, we begin to recognize the subtle signs and synchronicities that guide us. We develop what I call creative intuition—the ability to sense exactly when to act and when to wait, when to speak and when to remain silent, and when to push forward and when to let things unfold naturally.

The Power of Surrender

The act of surrender often makes modern women uncomfortable. We've fought so hard for our independence, our right to direct our own lives, that to surrender can feel like stepping backward. But I'm speaking of a different kind of surrender. One that does not involve giving up our power. I'm referring to the innate surrender within—an alignment with a greater power that flows through us. This is the surrender of the ocean to the moon's pull, creating the mighty tides. It's the surrender of the seed to the force that transforms it into a towering tree. This kind of surrender doesn't diminish our power. This surrender magnifies by connecting us to forces far greater than our individual will.

I witnessed this paradox through my own resistance to surrender. For years, I approached creation like a battle to be won through strategy and will. I believed that maintaining rigid control was the key to success. Even when this approach left me exhausted and disconnected, I feared that letting go would mean losing everything I'd worked hard for. The turning point came during a period of forced stillness after a serious illness. Unable to push and strive as usual, I had no choice but to surrender to the wisdom of my body's healing process. In that surrender, I discovered something remarkable: The less I tried to force things, the more naturally they resolved themselves. This wasn't just true for my health but for every area of my life.

Surrender, in the feminine way, means releasing our grip on how we perceive things should happen while maintaining a clear connection to our truth. It's about trusting that when we align ourselves with creative forces, what needs to emerge will emerge in its perfect timing. This doesn't mean becoming passive or abandoning our desires. Instead, it means shifting from pushing reality to dancing with it. We remain clear about our vision while staying open to how it manifests. Like a sailor working with the wind rather than against it, we learn to harness forces larger than ourselves.

This practice of surrender requires profound trust, not in external circumstances, but in the creative wisdom that flows through us when we step out of our own way. This trust develops through experience as we witness how things naturally align when we release our need to control every detail. Consider how a woman's body knows exactly how to give birth. The more she surrenders to this innate wisdom, the more smoothly the process unfolds. Fighting against it only creates tension and resistance. The same principle applies to all forms of feminine creation. Our role is not to force the process but to allow it to flow through us.

From Effort to Effortless Creation

The path from forced effort to effortless creation isn't found through trying harder. It's discovered through letting go. This shift begins with a simple but profound realization: Creation is natural to us as women. We don't need to learn how to create. We instead need to unlearn the habits that block our natural creative flow.

I see this journey clearly in my own life. I spent years pushing against reality. The results were always the same—exhaustion, frustration, and creations that felt lifeless because they came from strain rather than flow. Everything changed when I finally understood that my effort itself was the obstacle.

The first step in this transformation is recognizing when we're putting in too much effort. Our bodies tell us when we're in this masculine energy state through tension, anxiety, scattered energy, and physical depletion. When you notice these signals, pause. Take a deep breath. Return to your center.

The shift to effortless creation happens naturally when we realign with our feminine essence. This doesn't mean we take no action, rather, our actions arise from a different source. Instead of pushing from our individual will, we move in harmony with larger creative currents. Think of how you feel when you're in a natural flow, perhaps while dancing, making art, or being deeply absorbed in something you love. There's effort involved, but it doesn't feel like effort. You're fully engaged yet deeply at ease. This is the state from which feminine creation naturally emerges.

The key to sustaining this state lies in the regular practice of the principles we've explored throughout this book. Daily meditation connects us with deeper creative currents. Working with our breath helps us recognize when we're forcing rather than flowing. Staying rooted in our feminine center allows us to create from wholeness rather than lack.

Most importantly, we must trust the wisdom of timing. Masculine creation operates on linear time—pushing to make things happen according to schedule. Feminine creation flows in cycles, like the moon's phases or the seasons. When we align with these natural rhythms, we discover that everything has its perfect timing.

Remember, your creative power doesn't come from what you do, but from who you are. When you're aligned with your feminine essence, creation flows through you naturally as your presence itself becomes a creative force. In this state, you don't need to make things happen, you instead allow them to emerge through you.

As you integrate these principles, you'll find yourself creating more while struggling less. Your creations will carry more aliveness because they emerge from flow rather than force. You'll accomplish more with less effort because you're working with creative forces rather than against them.

The ability to create effortlessly by allowing yourself to become a clear channel for creative force to flow through you is your heritage as a woman. Trust this. Trust yourself. Trust the wisdom that moves through you when you surrender to your natural way of creating.

Sacred Reminders

✦ True creative power flows through your being,
   not from your doing.

✦ When you find yourself in strain, pause and return
   to your center.

✦ Trust the wisdom of timing as everything emerges
   in its perfect moment.

✦ Your presence itself is a creative force when
   you're aligned with your essence.

✦ Creation is not your effort, but your nature.

Presence Over Action:
The Power of Feminine Being

As you have been learning throughout this book, there is a profound difference between masculine and feminine power. While masculine energy manifests through doing and achieving, feminine energy works through presence and being. This fundamental distinction holds one of the most important keys to awakening feminine power in the modern world.

Many women today have been conditioned to believe that the path to success and fulfillment lies in constant action, striving, and effort. We've learned to measure our worth by our accomplishments, our busy schedules, and our ability to make things happen. Because women are good at making things happen, we manage families, households, careers, and care for extended families and communities, all at the same time. Yet this approach to power often leaves us feeling burned out, disconnected, and diminished, even when we achieve our goals.

What if the true source of feminine power lies not in what we do, but in who we are? What if our greatest impact comes not from pushing and striving, but from embodying our authentic feminine presence? This section explores how women can access a different kind of power, one that flows naturally from our centered, aligned state of being.

As we'll discover, feminine presence has a magnetic quality that naturally draws to us what we need. It has the power to transform environments, heal relationships, and create profound change, all without the exhausting effort of trying to control outcomes through action. When we learn to cultivate and trust our feminine presence, we tap into a power that is both effortless and profound.

The fundamental difference between masculine action and feminine presence lies in their very nature. Masculine energy is outward-directed, focused on conquering and achieving in the material world. It sets goals, makes plans, and takes strategic action to manifest desired outcomes. While this approach can be highly effective for men, it often depletes women who try to operate primarily in this mode.

Feminine presence, by contrast, works through magnetism and attraction rather than force. When a woman is deeply centered in her feminine essence, she naturally draws to herself what she needs without having to chase or grasp. Her very being becomes a force that organizes reality around her. We see this in nature. Take the flower. It doesn't strain to attract the bee; its very presence, its natural state of being, creates the magnetism that brings pollination.

This is why trying to succeed through masculine action

diminishes feminine power. When we're constantly pushing, striving, and trying to make things happen, we disconnect from our natural feminine essence. We become like a flower trying to chase down bees. Not only is this exhausting, but it's also far less effective than simply embodying our natural radiance.

The key to cultivating magnetic feminine presence lies in learning to trust and embody our natural state of being. This means letting go of the constant doing and allowing ourselves to simply be present. It means trusting that our aligned presence is enough—more than enough—to create the changes we desire in our lives and the world.

When we're centered in feminine presence, we naturally have a transformative impact on our environment and relationships. Just like how the sun doesn't try to warm the Earth, it simply shines, a woman centered in her feminine essence naturally illuminates and transforms her surroundings. This power of presence can heal relationships, inspire others, and create positive change without the need for force or manipulation.

The shift from doing to being requires a fundamental trust in feminine power. It asks us to believe that our presence alone, when we're truly aligned with our feminine essence, is profoundly powerful. This trust allows us to let go of the exhausting cycle of constant action and sink into our natural state of magnetic being.

As we progress through this section, we'll explore practical ways to cultivate this feminine presence and learn to trust its power. We'll discover how to recognize when we're operating from masculine doing versus feminine being, and how to make the shift back to our natural state of power. Most importantly, we'll learn to trust that our feminine presence by simply being who we truly are is more than enough to create the change we wish to see in our lives and the world.

The Power of Centered Stillness

One of the most powerful ways to cultivate feminine presence is through the art of centered stillness. This is not the anxious stillness of waiting for something to happen, nor is it the empty stillness of disconnection. Rather, it is the rich, magnetic stillness of a woman fully present in her power. Think of a deep mountain lake. Its surface may be perfectly still, yet beneath that stillness lies immense power and depth. This is the quality of feminine stillness we seek to embody. When we learn to be still in this way, we access a profound source of power that is distinctly feminine in nature.

Many women resist stillness because they've been conditioned to believe that worth comes through constant activity. We fear that if we stop doing we'll somehow cease to be valuable or lose our impact on the world. Yet the opposite is true. When we learn to be still while staying connected to our feminine essence, our impact actually increases.

That's because this quality of centered stillness isn't something we need to create or achieve. It's our natural state when we're aligned with our feminine essence. Just as water naturally becomes still when undisturbed, we naturally settle into this powerful state of presence when we stop agitating ourselves with constant doing.

The first step in cultivating this stillness is learning to trust it. We must trust that being still doesn't mean being passive or powerless. In fact, centered stillness is one of the most powerful states we can embody. From this place, we can sense subtle energies, receive clear intuition, and have a magnetic impact on our environment without effort. Consider how a woman's centered presence can completely transform the energy of a room without her saying a word or taking any action. This is the power of feminine stillness. It doesn't need to announce itself or prove anything. It simply is, and in that being, it transforms. This kind of stillness requires us to release the masculine habit of constantly trying to control outcomes through action. Instead, we learn to trust that our aligned presence naturally creates the right conditions for what needs to emerge. Like the still lake that perfectly reflects the sky, we become a clear channel for pure feminine power to move through us.

Through this state of centered stillness, we begin to experience how feminine power operates differently than masculine power. We discover that we don't need to push, strive, or force. Our very presence, when we're truly centered and still, becomes a transformative force in the world. This is the gift of feminine presence—the ability to create profound change simply through our state of being. As we deepen our capacity for centered stillness, we become more magnetic, more intuitive, and more powerfully present in every aspect of our lives.

Living from a Centered Presence

The true test of feminine presence comes not in moments of meditation or retreat but in the flow of daily life. This is where we learn to maintain our centered stillness while engaging with the world around us. It's one thing to access this state in silence and solitude, and a total other thing to maintain it while navigating relationships, work, and the countless demands of modern life.

Many women ask how they can possibly maintain feminine presence while managing busy careers, raising children, or dealing with challenging situations. The key lies in understanding that feminine presence isn't about withdrawing from life, it's about engaging with life from a different center of gravity. That's because when we're grounded in feminine presence, we naturally begin to move through our days differently. Instead of rushing from task to task, driven by external demands, we move from an internal rhythm. We find ourselves responding rather than reacting, creating rather than forcing, and being rather than doing.

Consider how this might look on a typical day. Rather than immediately jumping into action when we wake up, we might take a few moments to connect with our feminine essence, allowing our natural presence to establish itself before engaging with the world. This subtle shift in how we begin our day can profoundly affect everything that follows. In meetings or conversations, instead of feeling compelled to fill every silence or prove our worth through constant contribution, we learn to trust the power of our present, attentive listening. We discover that our centered presence often contributes more to a situation than our words or actions could.

Even in challenging situations, and perhaps especially in challenging situations, feminine presence becomes our greatest power. When others are reactive or tensions are high, our centered stillness can become a stabilizing force that naturally diffuses conflict and creates space for solutions to emerge. Now this doesn't mean we never take action. Rather, our actions emerge naturally from our centered presence instead of from anxiety, obligation, or the need to prove ourselves. We discover that when we act from this aligned state, even small actions can have a remarkable impact. Like dropping a pebble in still water, the ripples of our aligned actions extend far beyond their initial point of contact.

Likewise in relationships, we begin to notice how our centered presence naturally draws others into greater alignment. Without trying to change or fix anyone, we find that our own aligned state creates a field that supports others in finding their own balance. This is particularly true in romantic relationships, where feminine presence can activate and inspire masculine energy in a way that forceful action never could.

The key to maintaining this presence in daily life lies in remembering that we don't need to choose between being present and being effective. True feminine presence enhances rather than diminishes our impact on the world. In fact, we become more effective as we learn to trust and operate from this centered state of being.

Navigating Challenges to Feminine Presence

Perhaps the greatest challenge to maintaining feminine presence lies in our deeply ingrained habits of masculine doing. Even when we intellectually understand the power of presence, we may find ourselves automatically shifting into action mode when faced with pressure, uncertainty, or fear. This tendency is perfectly natural given how we've been conditioned. From our earliest years, most of us learned that problems are solved through action, that worth is proven through achievement, and that femininity itself is somehow less powerful than masculine approaches to life. Unlearning these patterns takes both patience and practice.

One of the most common challenges arises when we feel we're not doing enough. In a world that values visible action and measurable results, the power of presence can feel intangible or even indulgent. We may find ourselves doubting whether simply being present is really enough, especially when faced with urgent situations or others' expectations. Consider Tatiana, one of my students who struggled with this exact challenge. As a high-level executive, she was accustomed to solving problems through decisive action. When she first began practicing feminine presence, she felt almost guilty during meetings where she chose to remain centered and observant rather than jumping in with solutions. Yet she soon noticed that her centered presence created space for better solutions to emerge, often from unexpected sources.

Another significant challenge comes when we face resistance or criticism from others who are uncomfortable with feminine power. When we stop engaging in constant doing and instead operate from a centered presence, it can trigger those around us who are invested in maintaining old patterns. They may try to pull us back into masculine modes of action through criticism, demands, or emotional manipulation. The key to navigating these challenges lies in deepening our trust in feminine power. This trust isn't blind faith. It grows through direct experience of how presence affects our lives and relationships. As we continue to choose presence over action, we accumulate evidence of its effectiveness, which helps us stay centered even when faced with doubt or opposition.

It's also important to remember that maintaining feminine presence doesn't mean we never take action. Rather, we learn to discern between actions that emerge naturally from our centered state and those driven by fear, habit, or external pressure. When we act from presence, our actions have a different quality. They feel aligned and effortless, and often have far-reaching effects beyond what we could have planned.

Now, the journey of embodying feminine presence is not about achieving a perfect state. It's about continuously returning to our center, especially when we notice we've been pulled into masculine patterns of doing. Each time we make this return, we strengthen our capacity to operate from feminine power. We just have to make sure to return.

The Art of Sacred Return

In moving from theory to practice, there are several powerful ways to develop and sustain feminine presence in daily life. These aren't techniques to master so much as practices that help us remember and return to our natural state of being.

The foundation of feminine presence lies in our connection to our center. This begins with our breath and our body, particularly the area of our womb space, whether we physically have a womb or not. When we bring our attention to this area, breathing deeply and naturally, we begin to settle into our feminine essence. This isn't about controlling the breath, but rather allowing it to remind us of our inherent connection to life's natural rhythms.

Regular meditation becomes essential, not as another task to accomplish but as a sacred time to simply be. Through meditation, we cultivate the muscle of presence and learn to distinguish between our authentic feminine essence and the layers of conditioning that often mask it. Even fifteen minutes of meditation in the morning and evening can profoundly shift how we move through our days.

In daily life, we can practice what I call presence pauses which are brief moments throughout the day where we consciously return to our center. These might occur between meetings, before important conversations, or any time we notice we've shifted into masculine-doing mode. These pauses aren't about withdrawing from life but about reconnecting with our feminine essence before engaging again.

Physical practices that encourage flow and receptivity can also support feminine presence. Gentle movement practices like yoga, dance, or simply swaying with music help us remember the natural rhythms of feminine energy. These aren't about achieving perfect form but about allowing our bodies to express and strengthen our connection to feminine presence.

Our environment also plays a crucial role in supporting feminine presence. Creating spaces that reflect and nurture feminine energy—whether it's a meditation corner in our home or simply keeping fresh flowers on our desk—helps us to maintain connection with our essence. These physical anchors remind us to return to presence throughout our day.

Perhaps most importantly, we need to practice trusting the power of our presence. This faith grows as we witness the effects of operating from our feminine essence. It's helpful to keep a presence journal, noting situations where our centered state created positive change without forced action. These documented experiences become touchstones that strengthen our commitment to feminine power.

Remember, the goal isn't to maintain perfect presence at all times but to develop the capacity to return to our center with increasing ease. Each return strengthens our connection to feminine essence and builds our trust in its power. It is through this consistent practice that we discover that feminine presence isn't something we need to create or achieve. Rather, it's our default state when we remove the obstacles to it. Like water finding its natural level, our feminine essence inherently emerges when we stop trying to be anything other than who we truly are.

This is the ultimate gift of feminine presence: The discovery that our authentic being is not only enough, but is our greatest power. In simply being who we truly are, centered in our feminine essence, we become a force for transformation in our own lives and in the world.

Conclusion

The journey from constant doing to centered being represents one of the deepest transformations available to women in our time. As we have explored throughout this section, feminine presence offers a different kind of power—a power that transforms through magnetism rather than force, through being rather than doing.

My purpose in writing this book has been to remind women that the building of structures and systems has historically been men's work, and to explain that when we adapt ourselves too closely to this framework, we risk losing our unique way of being. Throughout these pages, I have expressed that our role is not to imitate masculine energy, but to infuse it with movement, nourishment, and transformative power. This is our unique contribution to the world—our unique form of existence. If we embrace this truth, we will not only preserve our essence but also offer the balance our world so urgently needs. Our power lies not in imitating masculine traits, but in fully expressing our feminine essence. All we need is the courage to welcome the change that brings us back to who we truly are.

This change is not only individual but also revolutionary. Every woman who chooses to act in alignment with her feminine energy helps restore balance in a world where power is overwhelmingly expressed in masculine form. Our inner balance and calm become a silent invitation for others to remember their true selves.

The path is not always easy. We will encounter doubt, resistance, and the pull of old habits. Yet every time we choose presence over action, stillness over striving, being over doing, we strengthen our connection to feminine power and create waves of transformation that reach far beyond ourselves.

For centuries, women have forgotten how to meditate, to practice breathwork, and to awaken their spiritual power. They have forgotten the immense strength they already possess. Until they pause and reconnect with the ancient life energy within them, they cannot realize their true potential. This book offers the practices that can carry us back to this place of wholeness.

Remember: you do not need to perfect these practices. It is enough to simply return to your center, again and again, trusting more deeply each time in the power of your being. Your authentic feminine essence is already complete. Your journey is only about clearing the obstacles that block its natural expression.

The "Next Level Woman" is the woman who returns to her ancient essence. She recognizes the difference between masculine and feminine, honors this difference, and transforms it with love. I am not claiming that this woman is superior to men. Rather, with her superpowers—such as creative thinking, the ability to hold multiple ideas at once, and the gift of seeing connections invisible to others—she reveals her original being in a world that does not always understand or value the beautiful complexity of the feminine mind. True freedom is the harmonious dance between masculine and feminine energies.

And I promise you: every woman can return to this ancient essence—the original woman within her.

Sacred Reminders

✦ True feminine power lies not in what you do, but in who you are.

✦ Your centered presence is a force for transformation without effort.

✦ Trust that being still doesn't mean being passive.

✦ Your authentic presence naturally magnetizes what you need.

✦ Return to your breath and body when you notice yourself striving.

✦ Create regular presence pauses throughout your day.

✦ Trust grows through witnessing the effects of your centered state.

✦ You don't need to maintain perfect presence, just keep returning to center.

✦ Your authentic being is not only enough—it's your greatest power.

✦ In choosing presence over action, you help restore balance to the world.

About the Author

With over 25 years of experience in the field of Behavioral Sciences, Nevşah Fidan Karamehmet is recognized worldwide as an authority in transforming dysfunctional thinking habits. She is the Vice President of the Behavioral Health Sciences Institute, the founding CEO of Nevşah Institute, and the founding CEO of the Breath Hub app, used by over one million people, which has trained more than 2,000 breath coaches.

Nevşah has traveled the world working with clients such as HSBC, ING Bank, Pfizer, and Vodafone, as well as renowned celebrities and professional athletes. She has given interviews on numerous radio and TV channels including BBC (UK), CNBC (USA), CNN (USA), and FOX TV (USA), and has been featured in publications such as TIME Magazine, Forbes, Telegraph, and Thrive Magazine.

www.ingramcontent.com/pod-product-compliance
Lightning Source LLC
Chambersburg PA
CBHW071740120626
46550CB00002B/600